Sheila Wray Gregoire is basically the "Dr. Ruth" for the church. And what a gift she is! Sadly, Christian women need to unlearn a lot about sex from what they've been taught in the church or in Christian books. Gregoire offers a thoroughly researched, biblically informed guide to great sex that is possibly more practical than conversations with your closest girlfriend. And she recaptures the meaningfulness, intimacy, and fun that sex is designed to offer your marriage. Every engaged and married woman needs a copy of this book!

Aimee Byrd, author of *The Sexual Reformation* and *Recovering from Biblical Manhood and Womanhood*

What a refreshing message for today's Christian woman. *The Good Girl's Guide to Great Sex* gives a Christian woman a biblical permission slip to desire and experience sexual pleasure and be a godly woman and wife. Woven throughout are deep biblical truths about healthy marriages, mental and physical roadblocks that derail sexual intimacy, tips to keeping it safe and fun, as well as some red flags signaling when a marriage may be unhealthy or toxic.

Leslie Vernick, speaker, relationship coach, and author of *The Emotionally Destructive Relationship* and *The Emotionally Destructive Marriage*

I thank God for Sheila Wray Gregoire. Literally. She speaks bluntly and honestly about sex but disarms with transparency, humor, and grace. This is a must-read for every woman who has questions about sex, which means this is a must-read for every woman. She goes where the rest of us fear to tread! I will be recommending this book over and over again

Sharol Josephson, director of FamilyLife Canada

This book has been my go-to bridal shower gift for years, and it's also my go-to homework assignment for Christian wives who want to work on their sex life. The updated edition is full of sound research that undergirds the practical and biblically based guidance that so many women didn't get while growing up.

Karissa King, MA, licensed marriage and family therapist and cofounder of the *Dear Young Married Couple* podcast

A delightful guide full of encouragement and information for women who want to create a beautiful and vibrant sex life. Every woman will benefit from this book.

Dr. Christy Bauman, author of *Theology of the Womb*

The

GOOD GIRL'S GUIDE TO GREAT SEX

The

GOOD GIRL'S GUIDE TO GREAT SEX

Creating
a *Marriage*
That's Both
Holy and *Hot*

REVISED AND EXPANDED

SHEILA WRAY GREGOIRE

ZONDERVAN
BOOKS

ZONDERVAN BOOKS

The Good Girl's Guide to Great Sex
Copyright © 2012, 2022 by Sheila Wray Gregoire

Requests for information should be addressed to:
Zondervan, *3900 Sparks Dr. SE, Grand Rapids, Michigan 49546*

Zondervan titles may be purchased in bulk for educational, business, fundraising, or sales promotional use. For information, please email SpecialMarkets@Zondervan.com.

ISBN 978-0-310-36478-8 (audio)

Library of Congress Cataloging-in-Publication Data

Names: Gregoire, Sheila Wray, 1970- author.
Title: The good girl's guide to great sex : creating a marriage that's both holy and hot / Sheila Wray Gregoire.
Description: Revised and expanded | Grand Rapids : Zondervan, 2022. | Originally published in 2012 as : The good girl's guide to great sex: (and you thought bad girls have all the fun). | Includes bibliographical references. | Summary: "Whether you're about to walk down the aisle or you've been married for decades, this revised and expanded edition of The Good Girl's Guide to Great Sex by popular blogger and award-winning author Sheila Wray Gregoire will lead you on a wonderful journey of discovery toward the amazing sex life God designed you for"—Provided by publisher.
Identifiers: LCCN 2021049385 (print) | LCCN 2021049386 (ebook) | ISBN 9780310364757 (trade paperback) | ISBN 9780310364771 (ebook)
Subjects: LCSH: Sex counseling. | Sex—Religious aspects—Christianity. | Women—Sexual behavior.
Classification: LCC HQ63 .G66 2022 (print) | LCC HQ63 (ebook) | DDC 306.7082—dc23/ eng/20211202
LC record available at https://lccn.loc.gov/2021049385
LC ebook record available at https://lccn.loc.gov/2021049386

The author is represented by MacGregor Literary, Inc.

Cover design: Curt Diepenhorst
Cover photo: Fuse / Getty Images
Interior design: Denise Froehlich

Printed in the United States of America

24 25 26 27 28 LBC 9 8 7 6 5

To Keith

I love you

Contents

Part 3: The Journey to Great Sex

Preface

Nobody grows up dreaming of being the Christian sex lady.

Talking about sex is weird in the first place. But speaking about it in front of hundreds of people, and blogging about it every day, and even doing podcasts with your millennial daughter where you talk about sex? That's super weird.

But somehow that's what I ended up doing.

I didn't plan on it. When I began blogging in 2008, I was a typical "mommy" blogger. I talked about parenting and housework and marriage. But every time I talked about sex, my traffic grew.

At the same time, my husband Keith and I were speaking at marriage conferences, and we were always roped into doing the sex talk because nobody else wanted to. Keith's a physician, so he'll talk about anything. And me? Well, I've always liked being the one who dares to go where no one else will.

So we began talking about sex more and more, and I became known as someone who didn't mind saying words like *erections*. People noticed. I was asked to do some magazine articles and a few TV spots on sex. And in 2012 the first edition of this book was published: *The Good Girl's Guide to Great Sex*. Copies flew off the shelves, and it became my signature book.

That was ten years ago. When I first wrote it, my daughters were seventeen and fifteen. Today they're both married, and they both work with me, talking about sex. I've given this book to all their friends as they've gotten married. I've spoken about this book in churches all over the world, including Kenya and Australia.

I've also written 2,500 blog posts since the first edition was published and received thousands upon thousands of comments. In 2020, together with two researchers (including my oldest daughter), I conducted the largest survey of Christian women's marital and sexual satisfaction ever done. We compiled the answers from twenty thousand women and were able to see how different evangelical teachings affected their marriages and sex lives. We followed that up with two more surveys, including one involving three thousand men.

Now, at the tenth anniversary of *The Good Girl's Guide to Great Sex*, I wanted to write this book again. Sex hasn't changed, but our conversations around it have. It's time for a new look at a very old issue. This is a major overhaul of the first edition, aiming to make it even more accessible and relevant to women who are just starting out on their marriage journey or who are trying to unravel what God meant for sex in the first place. I'm excited you're on this journey with me!

As we start this journey, I want to clear up one thing.

Whenever I speak about sex at churches, I always begin the evening by saying, "The problem with talking about sex from the stage is that I know all of you are sitting there in the pews, looking up at me, thinking, 'She must do it really well.'" But allow me to let you in on a little secret. Authors and speakers tend to write and speak into the areas of their lives that have been the most difficult. In our areas of difficulty, we have had to wrestle with God and grow, and so we have had to learn a lot. That's what gives us material to share! When we have struggled and cried and begged for help, and then come out on the other side with a fuller picture of what God wants, then, and often only then, do we have something profound to say.

I have had pretty awful sex. I have had amazing sex. And I have had sex that was kind of ho-hum. So no matter where you are as you embark on your journey, please know I've been there too. I hope that in these pages I can give you a glimpse of God's design for great sex and lead you on the most fun journey of discovery you'll ever take.

SHEILA WRAY GREGOIRE

Part 1

THE BEAUTY OF SEX

Introduction

Let's Talk Good Girls and Great Sex

This book is about one simple thing: how good girls and great sex can go together.

To some of you, that idea is exciting. I remember counting down the days until my wedding, and it wasn't because I looked forward to putting on my wedding dress. It was because I looked forward to taking it off! To others of you, the idea of good girls and great sex going together seems off-putting. You find the whole "good girls" talk a throwback to a bygone era when women's worth was measured in their virginity. For so long, the idea of being a "good girl" has been used to scare women into following rules out of a sense of shame or guilt. If you're a "good girl," you're better than the "bad ones." The definition of what makes someone a good or a bad girl has been limited to sex—whether we've done it or not, or even whether we like it or not! Some traditions think it's bad for women to like sex, some think it's bad for women *not* to. We women are in a tough spot!

What if that tough spot is not of God's making? What if God meant it when he called Adam and Eve, buck naked and not ashamed, "good" (Genesis 1:31)? And what if that pronouncement of good still echoes through the ages?

Okay . . . but what if you don't share God's enthusiasm? What if you can't quite pronounce yourself "good" because of shame about your sexual past? After all, great sex and guilt don't go together. They're like balloons and porcupines, hairy arms and Band-Aids, orange juice and toothpaste. Start sex with guilt and shame, and you'll struggle to enjoy the wonder of being together. Those damning messages make you feel like you've tainted your marriage before it even began. (That's a lie, sister, and we'll take it apart.)

Maybe you're staring down at that diamond on your left hand, knowing you'll soon be wed, but you're not sure you're ready to embrace your sexual side. Maybe you've spent your whole life trying not to get too excited and not think about sex. Or maybe you've even been abused or harassed and the sexual side of marriage seems ugly and even threatening, like it's a huge cloud you can't see through.

Then there are those of you who have already walked down the aisle, and the idea of *good girls* = *great sex* feels like a huge rip-off. You did everything right, and you were promised you'd reap amazing sexual rewards, yet you still can't figure out what all the fuss is about. (I hear you. That was me too. I've got you covered.)

Or perhaps you feel like your "good girl" status is a lie because you're keeping a secret. You want to experience a great sex life with your husband, but you struggle with porn or erotica. You find yourself fantasizing about strange scenarios or about strange men.

Or maybe you're a little confused and embarrassed. You're married, but you know there's something more. And you're afraid you'll spend your whole life missing it.

What if, before any of us can figure out the "great sex" part of the equation, we need to figure out that "good girl" part? Sex is a rich, deep experience between two people that is the pinnacle of intimacy, love, and pleasure. Great sex, then, starts with *you*, not only your body parts. You're the main part of the equation. And that's why our definition of a "good girl," which has been so focused on our pasts, has put us off track.

Great Sex Doesn't Require You to Be Something You're Not

My husband was bullied in school. He was a smart and sweet kid (which is probably why he's a smart and sweet man), and kids used to hassle him to copy his homework. He went on from public school to excel in med school, and he returned to his hometown as a pediatrician. Early in his career, when he walked into the delivery room, the prospective dad took one look at him and turned pale. "Please don't hurt my baby," he said. For there, before Keith, was the bully who had taken a swing at him fifteen years earlier. Now the tables were turned.

Keith had mercy on both the baby and the dad, and the day ended happily. But while Keith once felt like a weakling, that didn't mean he *was* a weakling. He had brains, he had motivation, and he had God to help him make it through med school (and an awesome wife who paid the bills). He may not have realized all his assets during his public-school days, but he was better off than the bully who acted so tough.

That's what it's often like with great sex. Our image of great sex and the reality of great sex are often two different things. You don't need to be someone other than who you are to have great sex. The more you are free to be yourself, confident in who God made you to be, the better sex will be. No pretense. No mask. Just *you*. The prototypical sexually happy woman likely looks less like a stiletto-sporting, club-hopping supermodel and more like that middle-aged secretary who lives down the street, puttering around in her garden, packing an extra twenty-five pounds. Gravity may have taken its toll, but she's the one who's the tiger in the bedroom. She's the one having fun because she has the secret to sexual success: she's been married to the same man for the last twenty-two years, and they're totally and utterly committed to each other.

Great sex isn't something that exists outside of you that you just "get" one day, like "getting" roses on your anniversary when the delivery van arrives, or suddenly "getting" algebra, when everything clicks. Sex isn't a thing, and it isn't a concept. It's an intimate experience between two people choosing to celebrate each other.

Embracing Your Sexual Side Doesn't Have to Be Gross

Our culture's view of great sex seems like something that's in the gutter rather than something that's in the clouds. Instead of viewing sex as the celebration of intimacy that a couple experiences together, we tend to view it as something crass. What is "sexy" is often defined in narrow terms—and it usually has nothing to do with intimacy or marriage. It's a woman with a certain body type, oversized confidence, and a repertoire of sexual tricks. But to have great sex, you don't have to be a pinup model, a porn star, or a woman with a ton of sexual experience. You can be you, bringing everything you are to the bedroom. Sexual confidence is far less about feeling like you understand sex and far more about feeling confident in who you are, individually and as a couple.

> Sexual confidence is far less about feeling like you understand sex and far more about feeling confident in who you are, individually and as a couple.

Our culture celebrates sex as instinct—we have a drive that needs to be met. TV shows feature women on the prowl, interested in the next sexual conquest. Women are portrayed as sex obsessed in pretty much the same way we think fourteen-year-old boys are.

I don't understand why this "sex as instinct" is supposed to be so marvelous, though. After all, animals operate on instinct too. Their goals in life—inasmuch as they're able to make goals—are simply to have their physical needs met. And by and large, they instinctively know how to do that.

People, on the other hand, have to be taught what to do. Then, even when we are taught, we have the capacity to refuse. We can act in ways diametrically opposed to our well-being. We can be stupid. We can be selfish. Yet we can also be noble, something most animals, except for a few dogs, aren't able to be. That's what makes us human: we have a choice. And because of that, we have the capacity to be good and to choose to do what's right. In other words, people *aren't* simply animals. We're higher than that. To think that operating solely on animal instinct is progressive is exactly backward. It's regressive.

And that's why good girls can have great sex. We don't try to be less than God made us to be, and we don't try to be anything other than what God made us to be. We embrace who we are—and share it passionately!

What If You Don't Feel like a "Good Girl"?

If you don't feel like a "good girl," please hear me on this: Jesus is pleased with you. No matter what you struggle with, once you've accepted Jesus's sacrifice for all the ugly stuff in your life, now when God looks at you, he doesn't see what you're ashamed of. He doesn't see the drunken parties or the groping in the back seat of someone's car. He doesn't see your quest for the next guy to make you feel alive. He certainly doesn't see you through the lens of what someone stole from you or how someone used you. When God looks at you, he sees Jesus's love, sacrifice, and compassion for the pain you've been through. He sees you as a good girl who has embraced the truly Good One who understands your wounds and bandages them up.

A good girl, then, is not someone who has done everything right or who has never had anything bad happen to her. On the contrary, a good girl is someone who knows and follows a good God—a God who sees her, not her past. A good girl is someone who understands that sex is good because God made it good and that her body is good because God made it good. When God created the world, he pronounced it good. When he created people, he pronounced his creation *very* good.

God thinks that sex is part of the goodness of enjoying each other. Great sex isn't just about X-rated sex. The best sex and the hottest sex is often between two married people who are able to let go and be naked and not ashamed (Genesis 2:25).

That is good news! You can be a "good girl" even if you struggle with sexual problems, are haunted by your past, or are simply trying to get over a deep-seated fear that sex is dirty. Being a good girl is not based on what you do; it's based on whose you are. Or, as I like to say, your goodness is not based on what you do with your body but on what Jesus did with his.

> Your goodness is not based on what you do with your body but on what Jesus did with his.

Maybe this idea of great sex doesn't make sense to you. You have no interest in being a good girl, you're happy the way you are, and you think this emphasis on sex with one person for life is a way of ensuring everyone feels guilty and no one has any fun. Will you hear me out? I think you're missing out on the amazing aphrodisiac that comes from true intimacy—an intimacy you were designed for.

I want you to experience that closeness because I want your marriage to thrive. In fact, I've always been passionate about healthy families. While most little girls daydream about their wedding, I wasn't nearly as focused on lace and satin. I tended to dream about being happily married with three or five or seventeen children. I didn't want the romance; I wanted stability.

I was raised by a single mom after my dad left. Growing up, I found so much hope in God's promises and ideals for what family and love should look like, and I wanted that for myself. In university I did postgraduate work in sociology, focusing on the family specifically, to verify that God's design for marriage really was the best. When I was still young, I married a man equally devoted to God and to having an awesome family.

And even though our marriage had a rocky start—as you'll hear about in this book—I never doubted my marriage because I knew my husband was awesome, I knew my husband was not the kind of person who would walk out like my dad did, and I wanted to do my part to see our relationship thrive. When my children were small and a window opened up for me to write for parenting magazines, I jumped through it. Within a few years, I was writing books on parenting, sex, and marriage, trying to share my own passion for families getting healthy. And over the last few years, my husband has joined me as we speak at marriage conferences.

What I learned in writing and speaking was that the more I understood what God intended for sex, the better sex was. Great sex is something you discover as you embrace yourself, embrace your spouse, and embrace who you are together. That's when things become explosive!

So welcome to your journey of sexual discovery. Whether you're married, engaged, or thinking about getting married; experienced or naive; abused and wounded or anxious but excited, God has a path for you that leads to deep connection relationally, spiritually, and physically. In what follows, I hope to help you find it.

CHAPTER 1

The Three Ingredients of Great Sex

You were created to enjoy sex. God made you just the way you are—with your anatomy, personality, and desires—and he created your husband (or future husband) with his own anatomy, personality, and desires. And then he designed you both to connect in an intimate, passionate, even chaotic embrace. Sex is not an afterthought on God's part—it's deeply wired into you, into the very center of who you are. You are a sexual being. God made sex to be so wonderful that for a few moments it's as if you and your husband are the only people who exist. Everything is supersensitive. Your senses are heightened. You lose control.

This is how God intended it. He wants you to be overcome with your husband, to experience that pinnacle of pleasure, and to feel truly and fully alive. I want to help you make this ideal a reality in your marriage, and I have a lot of tips and tricks coming! But first I want to set the stage because how we think about sex largely determines how much we enjoy it. So let's look at the three markers of great sex.

Great Sex Is Pleasurable

God created you with the ability to reach orgasm, the height of sexual pleasure where your whole body feels an intense rush and sense of release. And, as a woman, you have a body part whose only purpose is to provide that pleasure (in case you're wondering, that's the clitoris). Not only that, but women's bodies are capable of multiple orgasms, on top of each other, wave after wave. Not every woman will experience that, and it's not a prerequisite to being a successful lover or anything, but God created us with that potential. That means our pleasure matters! Sex is supposed to feel great.

Unfortunately, that leaves some of us with a problem. Many of us have rather awkward relationships with our genitals. In the movie *Fried Green Tomatoes*, Kathy Bates plays an insecure, introverted doormat. Everybody takes advantage of her, and so in defiance she joins a women's self-help group meant to boost confidence. This little mouse of a woman walks into her first meeting only to find the leader instructing everyone to take out a mirror, hike down their panties, and study their vulvas and vaginas. Mortified, Bates rushes out, hyperventilating all the way.

What would you have done?

Personally, I've been there, and let me share a bit of my background since we're going to talk so intimately in this book anyway. Today I have a great marriage, and we definitely have fun. But it has not always been that way. When I walked down the aisle, I carried a huge amount of baggage related to trust. I had been left by my dad as a baby, abandoned by my stepfather as a teen, and rejected just two months before my wedding by my fiancé. The latter man eventually changed his mind and came crawling back, and I welcomed him with open arms. Unfortunately, the rest of my body didn't cooperate. As much as I loved my husband and wanted to make love, I was scared to be too vulnerable, and my body wouldn't relax. And when you can't relax, sex can hurt.

This was in the days before pelvic floor physiotherapy was well-known, and because I came from a family of doctors, it was assumed that a physician was the answer to everything. So after confiding to a close family member about my problems, I was marched off to a gray-haired gynecologist who explained that I just needed to get in touch with my vagina. He would put me in stirrups, with my husband present, inviting me to touch everything and name everything so I wouldn't be scared of anything anymore. Apparently saying the word *vagina* is supposed to magically eradicate deep-seated trust issues and years of pelvic floor muscle spasms. And just like Kathy Bates's character, I hyperventilated and beat a hasty retreat, never to darken the door of that doctor again.

I eventually recovered from the pain without the aid of stirrups and physicians, but many of us aren't sure how to think about our body parts that are supposed to feel great or supposed to be sexual, because many of our interactions with those same parts have been, well, icky.

When my daughter Katie was eleven, her Sunday school teacher told her she'd have to stop wearing V-necks to church now that she was starting to develop, because adult men may stare at her chest, and she may become a stumbling block. She was so grossed out she didn't want to go to church for weeks. Many of us have grown up feeling like our bodies are dangerous, they're sources of temptation, they're somehow not quite right.

In one of our recent surveys, we asked women what terms about bodies and sex they knew before they finished high school. The results were rather abysmal. More knew the term *scrotum* than the term *vulva*.[1]

Why would young women know more about male body parts than female ones? I have a theory: Too often women's bodies are treated like trade secrets—they must be kept under wraps. Our bodies are not a legitimate subject for discussion unless it's to police how much we cover them. Our bodies are off limits. And what is off limits often carries with it a sense of shame.

People have always been suspicious of women enjoying sex too much because if we do, we may decide to have sex indiscriminately, stray from our marriages, or leave and disgrace our families. As a way of keeping girls from experimenting, families often taught them to be ashamed if they liked anything remotely sexual. They swatted girls' hands when, as toddlers, they touched between their legs. Families didn't tell girls the names of their body parts.

Even when parents try not to be negligent, we can still miss key things because we're not used to talking openly about girls' body parts or sexuality. I actually forgot to teach my own girls the words *vulva* and *vagina* when they were small. One day we were unloading groceries from the shopping cart into the car when five-year-old Rebecca piped up, with projection skills the envy of any on Broadway, "Mommy, why do you have hair on your bum?" I couldn't figure out what she was talking about. I was pretty sure I didn't look like a werewolf. Then I realized that my girls thought my "bum" went from the back around to the front and was the whole thing, like some giant basketball. I shushed her and buckled her into the van while fellow customers smirked.

I remedied the situation soon afterward and made sure my girls knew the proper anatomical terms because I knew that what we can't name often carries shame. But parents throughout history and across most cultures, instead of teaching girls that sex is truly a beautiful gift they were meant to enjoy, have tended to keep sex a shameful secret, not naming it, not talking about it, and hoping their daughters would never be curious about it.

I don't know what kind of relationship you have with your body, and I certainly don't want to imply that if you can't whip out a mirror and gaze admiringly at your genitals that your sex life is doomed. I've known women who could never work up the courage to insert a tampon who still figured out great sex, and I've known women who could carry on a conversation while soaping up naked in the YMCA showers who still had trouble reaching orgasm. Feeling comfortable doesn't guarantee pleasure, and feeling uncomfortable doesn't mean you'll never experience it. But embracing God's vision for sex involves understanding that pleasure is good. You don't need to be embarrassed or ashamed.

Keep Pleasure in Perspective

Embracing pleasure is awesome. But when we focus on pleasure and only pleasure, our message around sex can become distorted. Our culture's empowerment message to women when it comes to sex and our bodies sounds quite woman-positive. It says we need to take control of our own sexual satisfaction. We need to be in touch with our own bodies, know what we like, and celebrate our sexuality before we can have any sort of sexual relationship. The relationship itself is secondary to our own sexual selves. We need to know how to have an orgasm and know our own preferences before sex can be good.

The approach makes sense. In a world that doesn't believe sex should be confined to a lifetime commitment, it's assumed you'll have sex with many partners. The only constant in your sex life, then, is you. To get sex right, you need to research *you*. But in a marriage, you know you're with this man till death do you part. You have time to learn.

> What makes sex truly great is not only orgasm but relationship.

You don't have to know what's good for you right away; you get to learn what's good for *both of you*. Pleasure is important, but what makes sex truly great is not only orgasm but relationship.

When God said a husband and wife "become one flesh" (Genesis 2:24), he didn't mean it only physically. Sex has amazing power to bond us together in multiple ways, not only physically but mentally, emotionally, and spiritually as well. When we see it only as genitals joining, it can feel rather awkward and debased and make some of us want to hightail it out of there! But when we understand that it's much more than that, we begin to catch a glimpse of the bigger purpose.

Too often we get sex wrong because we think it's all about body parts: God created genitalia to fit together, and when you're married, you're allowed to connect the puzzle pieces. Sounds kind of silly that way, doesn't it? It's as if it doesn't have anything to do with the relationship at all but is just an "extra" that you get in marriage, sort of like "Do you want fries with that?" I don't mean to diminish physical problems that can make sex difficult or painful, and later in this book we'll go over some helpful strategies to solve some of those challenges. Yes, sex involves our bodies, and we do need to embrace our bodies and not feel shame about them. But sex doesn't involve only—or even primarily—our bodies.

Great Sex Doesn't Need an Amazing Body

I was recently driving near the busiest intersection in my small-ish town when a sign outside an herbal store caught my eye and almost caused me to go careening through a red light. "Breast enhancements—Buy 2, get 1 free!" I couldn't figure out where the third was supposed to go.

I soon realized that they merely meant bottles of pills. But the idea that bigger is better when it comes to boobs, while smaller is better when it comes to almost everything else, has so permeated our culture that we're left thinking we're inadequate if we don't have Barbie-like proportions.

Since our culture is obsessed with physical pleasure, it is only natural that it is also obsessed with "sexiness"—and sexiness defined in narrow terms. We think that a hot body is indispensable for hot sex. No wonder many of us suffer from low self-esteem. But guess what, friends: you can be sexy without photoshopping! You may be thinking, "That's fine to say, Sheila, but you haven't seen me naked." You're right. I haven't. And I don't particularly want to either. But our study of twenty thousand women showed that by far the biggest determinant of a great sex life was a great marriage. It's not about being 36–24–36. It's about loving someone and feeling truly valued and accepted.

Yet it's understandable that body image plays a huge role in how we think of sex. In our pornographic culture, where sex has often become about objectifying, dehumanizing, and using someone, we can easily cheapen what should be an intimate bonding experience. Because we minimize the aspects of sexuality that grow our souls and magnify those that have the capacity to shrink them, we're left with the suspicion that perhaps sex isn't beautiful. Sex becomes associated with something that is selfish, animal, and base, rather than precious, uniting, and sacred.

Look, sisters, there is nothing wrong with sexual feelings, and there's nothing wrong with enjoying your body. You were meant to enjoy sex. Yearning for your husband to take you, feeling excited when he looks at you, and even enjoying a quickie before work are all wonderful! Not every sexual encounter has to be imbued with great significance. But the sexual relationship itself should be something special, and all too often it's not. God made sex to be wonderful physically, but he didn't make it *only* to be wonderful physically. It's much more than that, which is what our culture too often fails to understand.

Great Sex Is Intimate

If an alien were to come to earth and see all our sex stores, he would invariably think that we must all have a lot of amazing sex. (I don't know why I picture aliens as male, but there you go!) In my small town we have a sex shop, two bondage stores, an adult video store, and two strip joints. When sex isn't about relationship, it becomes about how to make it as adventurous as possible. And what happens when your body gets used to physical pleasure for its own sake, without any commitment? You need more and more of the same stimulus to keep up the pleasure. Alcoholics need more and more alcohol to get the same buzz. Drug users need more drugs. The more we use, the more desensitized we become.

My friend Tracey didn't always understand this. Growing up, she embraced the idea that life was all about pushing the limits and having as much fun as possible. She worked hard, but she played harder. And she was as promiscuous as you could be in university. "I was always looking for the next greatest orgasm. I'd try anything once, hoping it would give me a new high because everything else was getting boring." Sex was physically wonderful, but it was never enough. It left her empty. She was always chasing after another guy, another sex trick, another position. Then one night she suffered a drug overdose and ended up in a Parisian hospital. She told God that if she got out of there alive, she'd try to figure out who he was. God gave her a second chance, and she honored her promise, big time. Now, almost thirty years later, she has a great marriage and pours herself into helping the homeless in our community. But many women are lost, as Tracey was, desperately seeking the next physical high.

Physical highs are wonderful, but they're more satisfying and more likely to be achieved in the context of marriage. And that's what God wants for us: both commitment and passion. If you're to experience awesome sex, you have to get this into your head: God created it. He didn't do it as an afterthought, thinking, "Well, they have to reproduce somehow, and as icky as this is, it's the best idea I've got." He created sex intentionally. He made it feel stupendous for both men and women. He gave us oxytocin, a hormone that releases during sex that makes us feel close to our husbands. He made it so that, in the most commonly used positions, we can look into each other's eyes and kiss each other at the same time as we're connecting in other ways. It's not only about feeling good physically or reproducing; it's also about cementing a husband and wife together as one flesh.

And it works! When Maggie Gallagher and Linda Waite, authors of *The Case for Marriage*, crunched the numbers from the National Sex Survey, they discovered that the women who were most likely to orgasm during sex were married and also religiously conservative—either conservative Jews, Catholics, or Protestants.[2] To me, this makes sense. Women have the best sex when in committed marriages. Conservative religious women tend to be in those types of relationships. They take marriage seriously, as do their husbands, so they feel cherished and loved. And hence they experience the most fireworks.

For women, commitment is the best aphrodisiac, far better than Botox, breast enlargements, or sex toys. That doesn't mean all married Christian women will have great sex. I sure didn't for the first few years of my marriage. But they are the most *likely* to have great sex, and if you're one of the married ones who has yet to discover the key to unlocking that sexual bliss, I hope this book will help. And to start, let's remember: sex is about connection, not cleavage.

> Sex is about connection, not cleavage.

Healthy sexuality is not only about our attitudes toward our bodies but also, and perhaps more importantly, about our attitudes toward God and our husbands. Sex is a relational thing that happens to involve our bodies far more than it is a physical thing that happens to have an impact on our relationships. And it only takes reading the first few chapters of the Bible in the King James Version to see this.

Sex Is a Profound Knowing of Each Other

I'm not normally a King James girl, but I have to admit there are some elements of Scripture that are easier to understand in the good old KJV.

One of those can be found in Genesis 4:1: "Adam knew Eve his wife; and she conceived." For those of you who grew up with the KJV, you probably remember snickering as a teen when that passage was read in church. "Oh yeah! Adam *knew* Eve! Riiight." We'd elbow each other and giggle. We all thought it was a euphemism, a way to obscure what was really happening.

But perhaps the Hebrew word translated "to know" wasn't God's way of being delicate but rather his way of being accurate. In Psalm 139:23, David wrote, "Search me, God, and *know* my heart; test me and *know* my anxious thoughts" (emphasis added). In that same chapter, verse 1, David said, "You have searched me, LORD, and you *know* me" (emphasis added).

The same Hebrew root is used in all cases: *yada.* David has just spent a chapter writing about how God knows us inside and out and how God is everywhere. We can't escape from him. He knows everything we do and think, and he planned our days before we were even conceived. At the end of this chapter, David's response is to ask for an even closer communion with God.

What does our relationship with God have to do with sex? The Bible uses the same word for Adam and Eve having sex as it does for us deeply and intimately knowing our Lord. Chuck Macknee, associate professor of psychology at Trinity Western University, explains that sexuality and spirituality are intimately connected: "Both are based in incompleteness and searching for wholeness. In sexuality, we're looking for connection and fulfillment in another person. But this is really the same reason we search for God."[3]

Sex is ultimately a longing, a passion, a deep desire for connection. God created in each of us a longing for intimate connection with him, and he made us long for each other in the same way, to mirror how he feels about us.

Let me put it this way; billions of people have had sex. I am not sure how many have actually made love. To have sex is simply to do the physical act. To make love is to connect on many other levels as well, which is exactly what God made sex for. He made it to help us truly "know" each other, in every sense of the word. He wants us to know each other physically, to memorize each other's curves and freckles and scents and likes and dislikes. He wants us to know what our spouse yearns for and what makes our spouse uncomfortable. But he also wants us to know our spouse's heart, mind, and soul. He wants us to be joined. That can happen only in an intimate, committed relationship, which is why people can have sex with many but can make love to only one.

Unfortunately, too many people don't even realize they're missing out on the best. When my oldest daughter was four, we attended a playgroup every day. One day the woman in charge asked the children, "What's your favorite food?" All the preschoolers offered variants of macaroni and cheese, ice cream, or hot dogs until one little girl, Victoria, shouted out, "Lobster!" Her father owned a gourmet restaurant, and she frequently dined on leftover lobster. She didn't know what macaroni and cheese tasted like. The other kids, though, were equally ignorant of lobster. They thought mac and cheese was scrumptious because it was the best of their experience. I suspect that many women settle for mac and cheese and miss out on delicacies because they don't know how great sex can be.

Listen to what one respondent to our sex and marriage survey reported: "I wish I had known that it really takes trust, commitment, and more trust to have a fulfilling sexual relationship. I never reached real fulfillment until I had all the above plus intimacy."

In a society that talks so much about the physical aspects of sex—that's all we have left when intimacy and connection are taken out of the picture—how can we understand what it is to experience love during sex? I think we have to go back to how we understand God and why he created sex the way he did.

We serve a triune God—Father, Son, and Holy Spirit. And he has made us to be triune people too—body, mind, and spirit (or soul). In sex we should connect on all three levels. Unfortunately, too often we focus only on the body. But we can also connect in our souls—a real spiritual union where we feel completely one, as if we are entering another person (that *yada* we talked about!). And then there's the mind. Connecting with our minds symbolizes the reaffirmation of the relationship, the nuts and bolts of what brings a couple together, the decision we make day after day to love our spouses exclusively. It's the reason we connect—the goodwill and friendship we feel for each other. Making love is a statement of that connection, a reiteration of the reason for a couple's relationship. Every time we make love to our spouses, we declare once again that we are committed to each other.

For millennia, Christians have understood this threefold nature of sex, though they may have phrased it differently. Thomas Aquinas, writing in the thirteenth century, called its purposes offspring, fidelity, and sacrament.[4] Offspring coincides with the physical aspects of sex. Aren't children, after all, the ultimate result of two people becoming "one flesh"? While sex may feel amazing physically, God also designed it to be the doorway into parenthood so that the physical could never be the only motivation. Because sex can bring children, two people should have a commitment first to protect any children who come. That's where fidelity comes in, the relational aspect to intimacy, where we reaffirm our commitment each time we make love. Finally, there's the component that Aquinas calls "sacrament": a spiritual union where the couple becomes one flesh in every way. Intimacy is more than physical; it's relational and spiritual too. That's the threefold nature of intimacy that makes sex so intense, and that complete picture of intimacy will frame how we look at the aspects of sex through the rest of this book.

Nevertheless, that threefold nature of intimacy is not what's often talked about in evangelical circles. I have read some popular Christian books about sex and marriage that make me rather uncomfortable, partly because they downplay the relational and spiritual aspects of sex and instead make it sound like sex is mostly about meeting a man's physical needs. Having sex whenever he wants it, however he wants it, to satisfy him so he doesn't stray—as if his straying is somehow your fault—isn't a biblical way of portraying sex. In 1 Corinthians 7:3–4, Paul wrote, "The husband should fulfill his marital duty to his wife, and likewise the wife to her husband. The wife does not have authority over her own body but yields it to her husband. In the same way, the husband does not have authority over his own body but yields it to his wife."

> You won't experience great sex unless you realize it's as much for you as it is for him.

When you are married, you both need to give and take. You should go out of your way to satisfy him, but he also should go out of his way to satisfy you! And that brings us to the last principle of sex that women need to embrace: mutuality. You won't experience great sex unless you realize it's as much for you as it is for him.

Great Sex Is Mutual

A thread in far too much Christian literature says sex is mostly about husbands, and so we wives need to make it fun for him. Do what he wants. Be his every fantasy. Yes, we do need to think about our husbands. Yes, we do need to be sensitive that in the majority of marriages, the husband may have a stronger felt need for sex than the wife does. Yes, we do need to initiate. But when we talk about how we need to satisfy his sex drive, we make the same mistake that our culture makes. We pigeonhole sex so that it's all about the physical and not about the spiritual or emotional connection that it's supposed to encompass.

If you focus only on meeting his physical needs, then you start to think of sex that way: sex is all about satisfying him, as if he's some sort of an animal. "Meeting his needs" sex doesn't bring the two of you together; it dehumanizes both of you. And that is not what God intended.

Unfortunately, part of the Christian church buys this message. They think that because the woman was created to be man's "helper," we have to help men in this area.[5] We have to relieve men's sexual tension. But if we go into marriage with that attitude, we miss the potential for sex to be something that binds us together beautifully. We miss out on the gift of sex as God designed it—to be a countercultural intimate knowing, rather than only a satisfying of a lustful urge. And seeing sex as a duty has the potential to do some serious damage to our own sexuality.

Sex is something beautiful that is meant for the two of you *together*. Instead of thinking of it as something you have to do to satisfy him, think of it as a journey of exploration that you take with him, where you get to know each other's bodies, explore each other, and look into each other's eyes. It's not only about his release; it's about the bond that unites the two of you. That bond makes you feel seen, loved, and cherished beyond measure. And that bond will not form properly if sex becomes only about satisfying him.

Women, challenge yourselves to make your sex lives the best you can. But sex is best not when you do it as often as possible solely for him but when you embrace everything that sex should be, and that includes a deep emotional and spiritual connection, along with real physical fireworks for you too. When you work on forging that bond, pursuing romance, and prioritizing your own experience, sex can be great. When you view sex as a chore in which you have to act all excited or your husband won't feel loved, you do great damage

> Fight for a sex life marked by pleasure, intimacy, and mutuality—and don't settle for anything less.

to yourself. You'll likely feel cheap, used, and resentful. Fight for a sex life marked by pleasure, intimacy, and mutuality—and don't settle for anything less.

How do we get there? We will look practically at this threefold nature of intimacy while troubleshooting what to do when common roadblocks pop up. First, we'll talk about the physical so that you don't miss out on the fireworks. Second, we'll talk about intimacy, the spiritual connection that makes sex hot and holy at the same time. And finally, we'll turn to emotional bliss, the ability to rest easy, knowing that your spouse truly knows you, cares about you, and sees you as you are—and you do the same for him. It's mutuality, it's vulnerability, and it's love.

Let's start by going back to the basics.

Part 2

THE THREE ASPECTS OF INTIMACY

Physical
Intimacy

CHAPTER 2

Great Sex Basics

When my daughter Katie was eight, she asked me that dreaded question: "Where do babies come from?" I took a deep breath and covered the essentials.

She crossed her arms and sighed. "I see," she said. Then she peered at me through squinted eyes. "How long does he have to leave it in for?"

The conversation went downhill from there.

The next morning at breakfast she threw her arms around me and said, "Thank you so much for doing that terrible thing with Daddy just so that I could be born." Obviously something was lost in translation. And I had to try to retranslate it for her.

In this chapter, I want to make sure that nothing is lost in translation. If you're engaged, you likely want to know how sex works. But even if you're already married and have already had plenty of sex, don't skip this chapter. It's always good to refresh ourselves on how our bodies are supposed to work.

Think of this chapter as the medical textbook side of this book. It's like a more detailed version of "the talk" your parents gave you when you were a child. But we'll also keep it clinical, so picture all this text being read to you by a Maggie Smith or a Judi Dench, speaking in an upper-crust British accent while wearing tweed and drinking tea. After we've covered the basics, we'll move on in other chapters to how to make sex more personal and fun. But first let's get this medical part straight!

Words about Sex Everyone Should Know

Before my friend Joanna was married, she didn't know how intercourse was supposed to work. She saw a skit on *Saturday Night Live* about tacos and wieners and hot dog buns, and that gave her more sex ed than she'd ever had. She assumed afterward that sex was like that—you move the wiener back and forth in a hot dog bun. Then one day, while browsing through a medical textbook as part of her microbiology university degree, she saw a picture of female genitals. She realized then that the vagina and the vulva were two distinct body parts and that sex was not about rubbing the wiener inside the vulva but instead penetrating the vagina.

Can you relate? Did you spend your teenage years surrounded

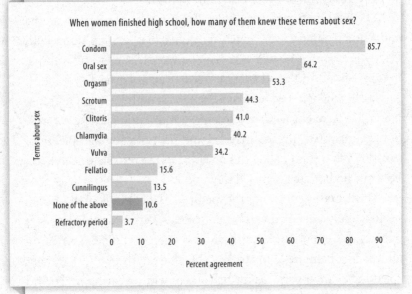

When women finished high school, how many of them knew these terms about sex?

Terms about sex	Percent agreement
Condom	85.7
Oral sex	64.2
Orgasm	53.3
Scrotum	44.3
Clitoris	41.0
Chlamydia	40.2
Vulva	34.2
Fellatio	15.6
Cunnilingus	13.5
None of the above	10.6
Refractory period	3.7

by everyone laughing at sex jokes while you awkwardly laughed along without understanding any of them? You're not alone! When we asked what sexual terms women could identify when they left high school, many were unfamiliar with an awful lot of them.

When I started speaking publicly about sex, I found it difficult to say out loud a lot of the words I'm about to tell you. I had to practice saying them in a mirror so that the shock factor wore off. But these words shouldn't be shocking. It's important to know our body parts and how they work.

The good news is you don't have to memorize these terms. There is no test. And I will not make you say them into a mirror or say them out loud—let alone in front of a crowd. I want to make sure you know what these terms mean so there's no confusion. Consider this your cheat sheet that will help you know what everyone else already seems to.

Vagina: Part of the female genitals. It is the muscular tube that leads from the cervix (the lower end of the uterus, or womb) to the outside of the body.

Vulva: The "outside" part of the female genitals. It includes the opening to the vagina, the labia majora (bigger, outer lips), the labia minora (smaller, inner lips), and the clitoris.

Clitoris: A small bit of tissue near the top of the vulva, close to where the labia majora meet. It is very sensitive to stimulation and can become more so during sexual activity.

G-spot: A theoretical area of highly sensitive tissue along the front of the vaginal wall. Its existence is debated, but many women report that receiving stimulation on the front wall of the vagina (the side toward her belly button) is pleasurable.[1]

Erection: When the penis expands and becomes firm. This results from neurologic signals that allow for increased blood flow to the penis. Other parts of the body, such as the nipples and the clitoris, can also become "erect" when aroused.

Sperm: The man's reproductive cell. It combines with the woman's ovum (egg) at fertilization.

Semen: Sperm plus the fluid they are suspended in. Seminal vesicles and the prostate produce this fluid.

Prostate: A gland that surrounds the base of the urethra (urine tube) in men. It makes a fluid that mixes with sperm to form semen.

Ejaculation: The expulsion of semen from the penis at orgasm.

Orgasm (or Climax): The peak of sexual excitement. It is accompanied by ejaculation in men and vaginal contractions in women. In both men and women, it is associated with intense pleasure. It is euphemistically called "coming."

Erogenous Zones: Parts of the body that respond to stimulation to produce positive sensations and sexual pleasure, typically (though not only) the breasts and the genitals.

Intercourse: Sexual activity where the penis penetrates the vagina. This can be done in a variety of positions.

Refractory Period: The period of time after ejaculation when a man's erection diminishes and he is incapable of having a new one. This varies and tends to last longer as men age but is generally around thirty to sixty minutes.

Foreplay: Touching and stimulating parts of the body (including erogenous zones) to achieve arousal for both. Women who orgasm during intercourse usually do so only after a significant amount of foreplay.

Oral Sex: Stimulation of the genitals with the mouth and tongue. It is euphemistically called a "blow job" when performed on a man. The technical terms are fellatio when performed on a man, and cunnilingus when performed on a woman.

Manual Stimulation: Stimulation of the genitals with the hand and fingers. It is euphemistically called a "hand job" when performed on a man. Most women find it easier to become sexually aroused from manual stimulation or from oral stimulation than from intercourse.

Masturbation: Self-stimulation of the erogenous zones to bring oneself to orgasm. Men usually do this by rubbing the penis up and down. Women often rub the clitoris, insert something into the vagina, and/or rub their breasts. Masturbation is a sexual act designed to bring one to orgasm; merely touching one's genitals is not masturbation. A child who rubs his or her genitals is not masturbating but exploring.

Sex and Procreation Basics

Now that the definitions are out of the way, let's figure out how all those pieces go together.

Here's what I couldn't fully explain to eight-year-old Katie when she wondered about the timing of his "putting it in." Intercourse is not just "insert tab A into slot B," as if you're assembling a bookcase. There's more to it than that.

When a man becomes aroused (or excited to have sex), his penis gets "hard" (erect) and protrudes from his body so that it's rigid enough to enter your vagina. His penis will also grow longer and thicker so that it's bigger than a penis in its normal state (flaccid, or soft). That's the "A goes into B" part. But that's only the beginning. When you're both ready for intercourse, he'll enter your vagina and then thrust back and forth, in and out, until he reaches climax (orgasm)—when he also ejaculates (releases semen)—or until you both decide to stop. There's a lot of movement going on, at least on his part (and, if you want to have fun, likely on your part too).

Pretty much every time intercourse occurs, a man will have an orgasm (ejaculate). And that orgasm means he releases semen (the milky white fluid that contains the sperm) inside you. Each ejaculation contains about one hundred million sperm per mL. Those sperm then take a journey, swimming up the vagina, crossing the cervix (the opening to the uterus), and entering the uterus, looking for an egg. Every cycle, about ten to fourteen days before your period, you release an egg—and occasionally several eggs—from your ovaries (ovulation). You usually don't feel this, although some women experience cramping.[2] Around this time your hormone levels change because your body is getting ready for pregnancy, so your body says, "Let's get it on!" Your uterus starts thickening its lining to make conditions perfect.

That egg takes a few days to travel down one of the fallopian tubes, where it remains viable for up to two days. If a sperm happens to come across this egg while it's making its way down toward the uterus, then—bingo!—conception occurs. If that embryo then travels down the tube to implant in the uterus, you're pregnant.[3] Pregnancy is possible only for about five to seven days each cycle. The egg lasts only about forty-eight hours, but the sperm can stay swimming for up to five days (they're rather persistent). Most of the month, pregnancy isn't possible, but for the five days before ovulation and for roughly two days afterward, you're fertile.

After ovulation, if pregnancy doesn't occur, your hormone levels change again, often leading to slightly less interest in sex for the next week or two, otherwise known as the luteal phase of your cycle. (That doesn't mean you can't enjoy sex—only that you may need more warming up!) Then, roughly two weeks after ovulation, give or take a few days, if conception hasn't occurred, your body sheds all that extra lining it's built up in the uterus, since it's not needed. That "shedding" is your period, which lasts three to seven days and contains anywhere from one teaspoon to five tablespoons of blood (3–4 tbsp, or 45–60 mL, on average). And then, of course, there's the cramping, which is often at its worst when you're in your teens and twenties, often gets better throughout your thirties and early forties, and then, once perimenopause and menopause start, can be unpredictable. Some women develop horrible cramping and other issues, and some women breeze through.

Before we jump into how to make sex wonderful in a variety of ways, let's cover the practical aspects of getting pregnant—or not getting pregnant. If a woman has sex without any attempts to use birth control and has intercourse relatively frequently, her chance of getting pregnant in a year is about 85 percent. But what if she doesn't want to get pregnant?

Planning Your Family

You and your husband should be on the same page when it comes to planning a family—or planning not to have one. But that can be thorny because this is quite a controversial subject. Talking about contraception on my blog always gets me into hot water because some people are adamant that any form of contraception is morally wrong. Others are adamant that anything that isn't natural is bad for your body. And then there are those who simply want as close to 100 percent effectiveness as possible.

Some women feel strongly about family planning. But here's the thing: this is between you, your husband (or fiancé), and God. I won't tell you what to do, but I will tell you all the methods and considerations so you can decide what's best for you.

Remember: picking a method with a lower effectiveness rate that you are more likely to stick to 100 percent correctly is often better than picking one that works better but that you may get sloppy with. Talk to your physician about what is realistic for you. Also, some forms of birth control should not be used if you have certain health issues (for example, women with certain types of migraines should not use oral contraceptive pills). This chapter should not replace the advice of your doctor. It is meant to give you a starting point for asking good questions and having those conversations with your man.

Natural Family Planning (NFP) and Fertility Awareness Method (FAM)

Many Christians, especially Catholics but also other traditions, feel that procreation (having babies) is an inseparable part of making love. Remove the possibility of pregnancy and, according to this philosophy, you diminish sex by making it solely about your own pleasure rather than something sacred that you entrust to God. Natural family planning takes care of these reservations because pregnancy is always possible, though if you do it correctly, it's not necessarily probable.

Those following NFP keep track of their fertile days and then abstain from sex during that time. How do you keep track? You can chart your temperature every day because it changes right around ovulation. Another option is to chart the amount and consistency of cervical fluid. A variety of apps are available to make this easier. Charting can be quite cumbersome, and you have to be diligent and regular so that you don't miss your fertility window. Online support groups for natural family planning can help you through it.

PROS

One of the benefits of natural family planning is that you'll be more in tune with your body. You pay more attention to your body's cues, and thus you can more easily figure out when you'll be moody, when you'll be frisky, and when you'll need chocolate to get over that hump. When and if you do decide to get pregnant, not only is there no medication to get out of your system but you're also so acquainted with your fertility window that it's often much easier to conceive.

Some couples choose to use this method not because of religious objections to contraception but because they feel it is the most natural. These couples may choose to use barrier methods (condoms) during the fertility week and then enjoy intercourse without barrier methods at "safer" times of the month. When you combine tracking your fertility window with barrier methods during your fertile times, we call it the "fertility awareness method," or FAM.

I know some readers may have religious objections to FAM. I personally believe that God created us with the ability to choose whether to get pregnant. After all, we humans aren't fertile most of the time. That means we can't get pregnant at random; we're capable of it only a few days a month. And God made our bodies so that they give signs during those few days. To me that signals that God decided to give us some choice over whether to get pregnant. And FAM seems like a good balance for those who don't want to use anything hormonal or permanent but still desire to choose the timing and size of their family.[4]

CONS

My husband, a pediatrician, often tells this joke: "Do you know what you call people who use natural family planning? Parents." There's some truth to that. To prevent pregnancy, you have to be diligent at both charting and abstaining. And this method requires you to abstain from sex for roughly one week in four, right in the middle of your cycle when your libido is likely to be the highest. Who wants to do that?

If you choose FAM instead of straight NFP, using a barrier method during the fertility window, then many of these cons disappear. Nevertheless, of all the contraception methods, this one requires you to be the most diligent, especially if you have irregular periods. If you fail to track for a few days, you may miss your fertility window.

Barrier Methods for Him (Condoms)

The thin latex barriers called condoms have been a birth control staple for generations. Unrolled onto the erect penis and worn during intercourse, they catch the semen so that pregnancy doesn't occur. They also protect against most STIs (sexually transmitted infections), so if an STI from a past relationship will continue to be a factor in your marriage, this would be the method of choice.

PROS

Condoms make sex far less messy. There's no leakage after sex, and they're also quite inexpensive. One reader reported overcoming her initial reluctance: "In my mind, condoms were what single men carried in their back pockets for one-night stands so they didn't get diseases. Thirteen years and four children later, my thinking is a little different. We've used condoms off and on this whole time and only became pregnant when I wanted to be." And here's another "pro" that another reader reports: "Condoms decrease sensation for my husband, which can help prolong intercourse—and that can be a good thing for me!" Plus, when and if you decide you do want to become pregnant, you just stop using them.

CONS

A barrier by any other name is still a barrier, and though that doesn't bother everybody, it does bother some: "It truly feels like it takes away from close intimacy. We felt cheated on closeness." It's also harder to be spontaneous because you have to pause what you're doing and root around in the drawer for one of those little square packages.

Barrier Methods for Her

A condom prevents the sperm from traveling into the vaginal canal. Women can also use barrier methods that allow the sperm to enter the vagina but stop them from passing through the cervix and entering the uterus. A diaphragm, which looks like half of a ball, can be inserted into the vagina and put in place covering the opening of the cervix, preventing anything from penetrating. Other single-use rings, similar to diaphragms, are also available. They look and feel almost like a flexible cup of superthick plastic wrap inside a circular plastic ring.

PROS

Diaphragms and rings have few side effects and can be inserted before you start sex so that it can be more spontaneous. Also, the single-use flexible cups can be used during your period (if the flow isn't that heavy). Some women find that using these cups allows for somewhat less messy period sex (although most women find the biggest drawback to sex during her period isn't mess but general discomfort).

CONS

The diaphragm has to be fitted by a physician, which some women find awkward. If the diaphragm isn't inserted exactly correctly, sperm can get past it. And checking that it is in properly isn't always easy. As a result, even with perfect use, over the course of a year, about one woman in eight will get pregnant if this is the only method they use. When it comes to the single-use rings, many women have reported difficulty fishing them out, which is a whole other level of awkward. But if you're someone who is comfortable using menstrual cups, and is quite used to extracting things from this particular part of your body, this may be a great method for you that allows mess-free and worry-free sex at times of the month that you might otherwise consider off limits.

"The Pill" and Other Hormonal Methods

Now let's turn to pharmaceutical options of birth control. Probably the most popular method of contraception, "the pill" is 99 percent effective at preventing pregnancy if used correctly. Taken daily, the pill's mixture of hormones prevents the hormonal spikes that trigger ovulation, thus preventing pregnancy, since no egg is released.[5] It can also increase cervical mucus, preventing sperm from entering the uterus. For seven days a month, the hormones aren't present, so you have what looks like a period, though the flow is often lighter. "The pill" is a misnomer because there are plenty of variations of the pill with different doses of various hormones, so if one doesn't match well with your body, another one might.

If you don't want the bother of daily pills, you can use the hormonal ring, which is inserted in your vagina and left there for several weeks. A hormonal patch that excretes hormones into your body can also be placed on the skin. In these cases too, your period will be lighter.

PROS

Hormone therapies are very effective at preventing pregnancy, and they also minimize acne, PMS, and cramping. They're also used to treat certain conditions, including polycystic ovarian syndrome. One of my friends said, "The pill made me gain weight and get emotional, but it was perfect for the early days of marriage. No other method really worked because my cycles weren't regular."

CONS

The pill must be taken daily and at the same time. If you miss a pill, your body may ovulate, even if it's not the middle of your cycle. There's also the simple cost factor. The average pill costs about $1.50, and it must be taken daily, whether you have sex or not. The pill's hormones also work against the natural cycles that cause your libido to surge in the middle of the month. One study of 1,086 German female medical students found that those on the pill were far more likely to suffer from low libido or other sexual problems.[6] Also not so happily, hormone therapies have been linked to weight gain and moodiness, which are never a good combination. Even worse, they've been linked to blood clots and strokes in some women, and potentially breast cancer, although the chance of this is very low. Finally, the manner of stopping the contraception varies based on the type of hormones involved and the method of administration, and it may take a few months for normal cycles to return. This can delay getting pregnant when you do decide to have a baby.

One of my commenters reported her feelings about the pill like this: "After going off the pill, I realized the chemically induced roller coaster of emotions I was on monthly. I would never for any reason go on it again." Others love it. So my final thoughts: investigate hormonal therapies before you let the doctor write that prescription. I find that my blog readers either love the pill (it made sex so easy!) or they hate it (I had no libido and constant headaches!).

Intrauterine Devices

An intrauterine device (IUD) is a small T-shaped device made of copper or plastic that is placed inside the uterus by a trained health-care provider. IUDs work by thickening cervical mucus, which makes a barrier against the sperm. Also, copper is spermicidal, and the plastic versions release small amounts of hormones that can prevent ovulation. There was concern previously that at least some of the way in which the IUD worked was to prevent implantation after fertilization. This is obviously of concern to people who believe that life begins at conception. But the most recent research indicates that IUDs prevent fertilization, not implantation.[7]

PROS

Of all forms of contraception, the IUD provides one of the lowest pregnancy rates. Once inserted, it requires no further maintenance and can last from three to ten years depending on the model. Once it is removed, fertility goes back to normal quite quickly, and you can try to get pregnant right away

CONS

Some women find that their periods are heavier with copper IUDs, though some women's periods stop entirely with plastic ones. The biggest drawback is that a trained practitioner needs to place and remove it, and that procedure does cause some discomfort (which is a nice way of putting it!). But it is considered safe and can be done in your healthcare provider's office.

Permanent Birth Control

If you're sure your childbearing days are behind you, he can opt for a vasectomy (where the tube carrying the sperm is cut), or you can opt for a tubal ligation (having your fallopian tubes cut, then tied off so that the egg can't travel from the ovaries to the uterus). Although these procedures can be reversed if someone changes their mind, the chance of fertility returning decreases over time, so think hard before you decide on either of these procedures.

A vasectomy is a quick procedure that can be done in a doctor's office, while a tubal ligation is more invasive and requires surgery. His tubes are easily accessible; yours are on the inside. So the procedure is much easier if a husband gets it than the wife.

Which One Should You Choose?

Now that you know the array of options for contraception, how do you decide what to do? Talk to your fiancé or husband about it. Pray about it. Talk to your doctor. But I'll give this wise commenter the last word: "No birth control is perfect for sexual enjoyment, preventing pregnancy, or interacting with a woman's body. The key is to find the one that works the best for you." Exactly!

Now that we have the medical stuff out of the way, let's turn to how our bodies were made to respond to sex and enjoy sex.

CHAPTER 3

Lighting the Fireworks

Our family has had the privilege of visiting a children's home in Kenya, leading medical teams and learning from the residents about grace and resilience amid trauma and poverty.

While most of the students speak English, the smallest children usually do not, and we're left with communication roadblocks. That's why we always come equipped with bubbles, the universal language of toddlers.

Their favorite bubbles are the big ones that float gently and take longer to burst. But blowing such bubbles takes practice. If you blow too hard, the bubble breaks. If you blow too fast, small bubbles form rather than one big one. You have to start by blowing hard, but then, when the bubble starts to form, you need to back off and blow softly and evenly so that it expands until—poof!—you give it just enough oomph to break free and float.

You have to constantly make adjustments based on what the bubble seems to need.

Great sex is kind of like blowing a big bubble: You don't want to go too hard, or it will fizzle; you don't want to blow too fast, or the momentum won't build. You need to feed the momentum and react to the momentum and nurture the momentum. Yes, there's technique. But it's more about *paying attention and doing what needs to be done in the moment.*

That probably sounds confusing, right? Women on my blog often plead, "But I'd rather have specific instructions so I know exactly what to do!" In this chapter, I'll certainly give a lot of techniques that many women enjoy. But ultimately great sex isn't a paint-by-numbers process I can teach you. It's about *you* learning to listen to your own body.

Many women can attest to this experience: he does something to you one night that has you in raptures, and then three nights later, he does exactly the same thing, move for move, and you lie there thinking, "Can you just get it over with? I want to get to sleep!" Great sex is far less about what he's *doing* and far more about what you're *thinking*. It's not that technique doesn't matter. But the biggest factor in women feeling good during sex is learning to allow ourselves to feel pleasure—and then feeding that pleasure!

Unfortunately, this often isn't the way we approach sex. Instead of asking, "What does my body want right now, and how can I feed that feeling?" we ask, "What's the next step we're supposed to do?" We treat sex like a checklist rather than an experience.

I want you to experience great sex! I hope your toes curl, you want to scream in passion, and your body cries out to be touched. In the next few chapters, I'm hoping to help you get there—because sex *should* feel amazing! So let's zero in on the way God designed our bodies to *experience* sex, rather than just to *do* sex. To begin, let's take a step back in time.

Understanding What "Good" Feels Like

Why is it that parents worry so much about teenagers making out? Are we paranoid about the kissing itself? Nope, not usually. Instead, it's that we know that when you kiss passionately, after a while your body starts to want more. Certain areas of your anatomy might feel like they're on fire. They want to be touched. So hands naturally start exploring. That makes the fire even bigger. And the long, drawn-out make-out session gets our teenage lovebirds so aroused that they do things they weren't planning on.

That's how arousal works. We touch and kiss, and doing so wakes up our bodies. Before long, other parts want to be kissed and touched, and then hands wander and excitement builds until finally we reach orgasm.

Our bodies are meant to respond in a certain order. I want you to understand that order because great sex is a progression from one step to the next. Orgasm for women is mostly about learning the skill of listening to your body, knowing when to ramp up the stimulation, and then riding that wave of pleasure to take you even further along. It's almost like a surfer riding a wave!

To put it in technical terms, the sexual response cycle tends to look like this:

Excitement → Arousal → Plateau → Orgasm → Resolution

There's also a mental aspect to the sexual response cycle—desire—that we'll talk about more in part 3. But for now, let's focus on the physical steps to arousal, learn what each of these stages feels like, and then focus on how we can "feed" that pleasure so you can feel amazing! That means getting clinical again (I believe you can handle it!) so you can understand how your body was designed to work.

Excitement Phase for Her

Consider the excitement phase as your body's "waking up" time. Your body realizes, "Oh, hey, sex is on the table! That sounds like fun!" This phase focuses on gentle, tender, loving actions that help you mentally step out of "work/stress/mom" mode and relax into "feeling like a woman" mode. It could involve running your fingers along each other's arms, necks, shoulders, backs, legs, and so on or giving back rubs while you talk about your days. It could involve snuggling while you trace your fingers over each other, then moving to kissing and some sexier touching.

Some women describe this as getting "turned on" (although the actual physical signs of arousal happen more in the next stage). One woman explained,

> My husband and I were clueless virgins when we got married. I read your books and blog and followed your advice about asking myself if it felt good. The problem was that I didn't know what "good" felt like, so when my husband asked or I asked myself mentally if it felt good, as long as it didn't hurt, I said yes. My aha moment came when we were making out one time and I started having a feeling that I had gotten a few times before when I was younger and reading Christian romance novels. Embarrassing but true—I got aroused from that stuff but didn't have the language or awareness to identify what was happening when I was younger. It felt like a warm heartbeat in my clitoris that spread outward. So when I began to feel that with my husband, I wondered if that was what "good" meant. I focused on what was causing me to feel that way and what would intensify that feeling, and that's how I figured out how to orgasm. Once I knew what "good" felt like, I was able to listen to my body and learn what different things made me feel that way, and it got easier with practice.

"A warm heartbeat in my clitoris that spread outward"—that's a great way to describe it! Other women talk about a "tugging" feeling in their clitoris or vagina or even their nipples. That tugging feeling is blood rushing to those body parts, which makes them more sensitive—and makes them feel like they want to be touched.

You can feel turned on even when nobody's touching you, as this woman did while reading romance novels. It might happen while you're watching a movie and the couple finally kisses for the first time (after a frustratingly long lead up!) or when your husband (or fiancé) first looked at you or first kissed you.

As your body starts to feel warm, or you feel that tugging, your body experiences more changes. Your breathing becomes faster; your nipples harden. And you even get your own erection! Blood rushes to the clitoral region, and your clitoris becomes engorged and protrudes. Plus, you get wet. Women's bodies are designed so that when we're aroused, the vagina produces fluid, which makes your genitals slippery so that it's easier for the penis to enter and move around—and more pleasurable too!

Excitement Phase for Him

For guys, excitement can be categorized as a "start your engines" phase. Like you, his breathing and heart rate grow faster. His scrotum begins to tighten. But the most obvious sign is that blood flow increases to the penis, resulting in an erection. When a guy becomes sexually excited, the blood rushing to his penis causes him to become hard and erect, standing at a thirty- to ninety-degree angle from his body, or between 1:00 and 3:00 if you're looking at him while he's turned to your right. That's the perfect angle for making love, which is why he's made that way. He can enter you while lying right on top of you (or while you're on top of him, facing him), which makes it more intimate, since you can kiss and look at each other at the same time. And he becomes hard pretty much instantaneously. He springs into action and is ready to go!

By the end of the excitement phase, you're both ready to move on to more direct sexual stimulation in the arousal phase.

Arousal for Her

Once you've felt some excitement and your body begins to change, you want more direct stimulation on specific erogenous zones, like your breasts and clitoris or vagina. Your breathing and heart rate increase, and your areolas (the areas around the nipples) swell as well. What's often erotic and pleasurable at this stage is the build-up—if he starts at your feet and then kisses up the insides of your legs moving toward your genitals or starts at the belly button and moves up to your breasts or down to your clitoris. He doesn't have to treat the erogenous zones like a bull's-eye to aim for! He can treat them instead like a treasure map where he spends his time going *everywhere but* until he finds what he's looking for.

Arousal for Him

The arousal phase in men is pretty much more of the same: muscle tension heightens, the heart rate and breathing continue to increase, and the firmness of his erection may increase.

Plateau for Her

Up until now your physical arousal levels have been building, and you've become more and more "turned on," or desperate for sex. But right before orgasm, arousal stops growing and stays at the same level while your body waits for intense stimulation to put you over the edge. During excitement and arousal, you likely enjoy being teased with different techniques, changing things up, changing positions—all helping to build excitement and arousal. Once you've reached plateau, though, you'll likely find that consistency works best. If you've found something that makes you feel good, don't stop! Keep doing it to the same level, the same pressure, and the same speed until you reach orgasm. The main physical change signaling the plateau phase is that your clitoris "retracts," or goes flat against your body. At this point, your clitoris gears up to be stimulated through pressure (such as his pubic bone hitting your clitoris when he thrusts) rather than from rubbing it. When plateau is reached, many women prefer pressing on the clitoral region rather than rubbing back and forth.

Plateau for Him

For many men, the key is learning to make the plateau phase last longer so that he can help bring you to orgasm. During this phase (and even earlier in the response cycle), men can release small amounts of semen, called pre-ejaculate, which do contain sperm. Though the quantity of sperm isn't large, pregnancy is still possible. That's why the withdrawal method isn't on my list of contraception methods.

Orgasm for Her

When you reach orgasm, you likely know it because you feel an intense buildup followed by an incredible physical rush that washes over you in waves. You feel your vaginal muscles squeeze involuntarily and rhythmically (a woman's orgasm was designed this way because your contracting muscles end up squeezing him when he's inside you, which in turn helps him to reach orgasm and thus achieve pregnancy), and your head may thrash around. Your legs go stiff, and your pelvis automatically tilts forward (to allow the guy maximum penetration at that time).

When I was young, my mom gave me a children's book that compared an orgasm to a sneeze, which builds and builds until your body finally lets it out. I never liked that analogy much because I hate sneezes. But there is something to it: your body builds tension—sexual tension in this case—and wants to release it.

Your orgasm can last a long time, with multiple ones on top of each other (though this often takes some work to learn how to experience). You can also keep enjoying sex even after you've orgasmed, while men can't because they have a refractory period where they lose their erection and can't get erect again for a while.

Some women are surprised that during orgasm, liquid can suddenly be released in a rush. Many a woman has worried that she just peed or something. But don't fret—you didn't! Women can "ejaculate" at orgasm too, though this isn't terribly common, and it certainly isn't necessary. Some women enjoy it and find the orgasms more intense, but many women don't do this and still find orgasms great. If you experience this, use some towels, have fun, and roll with it!

Orgasm for Him

His orgasm is much more visible and obvious. His pelvic floor muscles contract about twelve to fourteen times in quick succession, and he ejaculates and releases about five milliliters (a teaspoon) of semen (it looks white and filmy). That may not sound like much, but you'll want to have a towel handy for afterward, unless you're using a condom. Some men remain at least partially erect for a few minutes after orgasm and can continue intercourse until she reaches orgasm. After orgasm, he won't be able to get aroused again for about another thirty to sixty minutes.

The Only Route to Orgasm Is through the Rest of the Cycle

I'm not going to test you on what you just read, and if you forget some of it, don't fret. But there is one thing I want you to remember: *your body won't magically get to orgasm unless it moves through excitement and arousal first.* That's why the route to orgasm isn't through doing specific actions; rather, you have to pay attention and not switch to something more intense until your body asks for it. Let your body be your guide.

Okay, that's all well and good. But what exactly is it that you're supposed to do to help you move through these different stages? What actually feels good? Let's explore that next!

> Your body won't magically get to orgasm unless it moves through excitement and arousal first.

How to Make Foreplay More Fun

Making foreplay fun is far less about doing something specific and far more about not jumping to the "main event" too quickly. It's making sure you move through the excitement and arousal stages so you can orgasm. Spend time exploring, figuring out what both of you like. It's relaxing and helps make intercourse more enjoyable. Even after you know each other's bodies, you should still spend most of your time in foreplay because that's how you jumpstart the sexual response cycle.

Not only that, but women tend to take much longer to reach orgasm than guys do, especially at the start of the marriage. If he can touch you and take his time and help you to relax and drive you crazy beforehand, then you'll likely enjoy intercourse a whole lot more.

To be really arousing, foreplay should resemble a tour of an exotic island rather than a treasure dig at a specific place. Sometimes guys think that foreplay just involves rubbing the clitoris, but it should be more than that. If he touches and kisses and nibbles you all over, and you do the same for him, you'll be more aroused and feel more intimate. I've heard women declare, "I don't like foreplay," but I often wonder if that's because their husbands are rushing it or not exploring quite enough. If you're dry because you're nervous or because you're preoccupied and it's going to take some time to get you in the mood, then having him rub your clitoris can be, well, annoying. Encourage him to pay attention to your whole body. And it's easier for him to want to do this if you also pay attention to his whole body. Reciprocate!

Now I seriously don't want to give you a step-by-step guide to what to do in foreplay, friends, because we all like different things. Explore and make up your own routine. Figuring it out is half the fun. What I would suggest is that you gear yourself up to talk to him about it early in your marriage, even on your wedding night. Don't start your marriage without sending clear signals about what you like because you'll find it hard to ask him to change later. The first time you're naked together, with only those wedding bands on, start communicating. Words aren't even necessary! If he's doing something you don't like, gently guide his hand to where you want it. Make reassuring sounds if he hits a hot spot. You may not even know what you want him to do, but as you become aroused, you'll find that certain areas of your body yearn to be touched. Guide him to those areas.

Incidentally, communication is perhaps even more important for couples who had sex before they were married. Just because you've had sex doesn't mean you did it well or that you enjoyed it. If it hasn't been overly satisfying, it's even more important to have open communication at the beginning of your marriage to make it better. You have a new start; take advantage of it. And if you've had sex in the past with other guys and something felt good, don't assume that the same thing will feel good with your husband. Try to launch into marriage with a blank slate, and learn what feels good when he does it. Let it be something you experience together with no preconceived notions. You may find that you like something with him that you never thought you'd like with anybody!

Now let's turn to how to drive each other wild.

What Makes His Toes Curl (and Other Things Grow!)

Guys tend to be ready to get busy right out of the starting gate. But just because men are ready to go doesn't mean they wouldn't enjoy a little effort on your part to make them feel even better. Besides, it's awfully fun to explore your beloved's body, and it can make you feel sexually powerful when you see the effect you have on him.

So what parts of his body feel the best?

Let's start with the obvious. Your husband's main erogenous zones are his penis and his scrotum (the sack that holds his testicles, hanging down behind his penis).

But what do you do with a penis? If you haven't seen an erect one before, it isn't like a tube, where it's the same thickness all the way up. The penis has a head where it's a little thicker at the top. In uncircumcised guys, this head is covered with the foreskin, which can be pulled back a little bit. In both circumcised and uncircumcised men, the most sensitive parts of the penis are the head itself and the rim, or ridge, right below the head. There's also a slightly enlarged area called the frenulum, right below the rim where the foreskin is attached (if the man is uncircumcised) on the underside of the penis (or the side that faces down when he's erect). Most men also find that deliciously sensitive. When you do touch him, ask him where it feels best. And let him show you how to touch him. You'll catch on.

Interestingly, you have that ridge on your clitoris too. You'll find that under the top part of your clitoris there's a little rim before the clitoris gets narrower, and that rim is more sensitive than the rest. When embryos are developing in the womb, the clitoris and the penis form the same way initially, differentiating themselves only later. So if you want to have an understanding of what parts of his penis feel good, you can often figure it out by what parts of your clitoris feel good.

The scrotum is also very sensitive, and many men like their testicles to be stroked or squeezed. But keep in mind how much guys hurt if they're kicked there. Don't be too rough! Ask him to show you what kind of pressure to use.

Men also find it arousing to have their nipples stroked or licked. And your husband probably has other body parts, like his ears or elbows or toes, where he would love to receive attention to drag out the encounter. His whole body is yours once you're married, so have fun exploring. And how should you explore?

KISSING

You've likely already kissed his mouth before you were married, but have you kissed passionately? Explore his mouth, suck on his lip or tongue, and get creative. There is no right or wrong.

Kissing doesn't have to be limited to mouths either. Kiss his neck and his chest. Kiss his nipples. And you can even kiss his penis if you're comfortable with it. Don't worry about pee either. Once a guy is erect, he is physically unable to urinate. Also, his penis is covered in the same skin as the rest of his body, and if he washed, kissing his penis is really no different from kissing any other part of his body. It's also a big bonus that there's no hair on the actual penis, unlike his chest and legs. And when you use more than just your hands, you learn how his penis feels and responds.

NIBBLING

Kissing is gentle. Nibbling is playful and a big turn-on for many men. But be careful where you nibble. The penis and the scrotum are very sensitive, and it's best to keep teeth away from those areas. Stick to nibbling earlobes, shoulders, and his chest, where he can enjoy the combination of teasing and a little bit of pain.

TOUCHING

Don't hesitate to touch him all over. Use your fingertips to memorize his contours. Run your fingers from his toes up to his head. Pay special attention to his penis, and learn what it feels like and how it reacts. He'll appreciate the effort!

SQUEEZING

If you've ever been aroused without having sex—say, after waking up from a graphic dream—you may have experienced the sensation of your clitoris being so aroused that it hurts. It wants desperately to be touched. That's what a guy's penis feels like too. And what often feels best is to squeeze—and squeeze hard. Let him show you.

One thing that often surprises new couples is how differently men and women like to be touched. Women often need touch to be more *delicate* (especially as they're warming up); men often need it more *deliberate*. Chances are that he'll be too rough when touching you and you'll be too gentle when touching him because you won't recognize how each other's bodies work. If you touch his penis the way you want him to touch your clitoris, it will feel more like teasing to him.

> # Women often need touch to be more *delicate* (especially as they're warming up); men often need it more *deliberate*.

These aren't steps you have to memorize to do right. You don't need to bring a primer to bed with you. All you need to remember is that there are many ways to explore his body, and you should feel free to do so as soon as you're comfortable. And then let him be your guide. He will be thrilled with the request.

What Makes Your Toes Curl

Just as guys have specific areas that produce major sparks when you give them some attention, so your body has parts that cry out for attention too. But not everyone has the same sensitivity in the same areas. I'm going to give you a road map of where most women are sensitive. If your husband explores all these areas, you'll probably find that some are winners.

Remember that in the beginning of any sexual encounter, in the excitement phase, you're trying to get your body ready to be turned on. So with women, it's important to start slowly and build up. Let's see what that may look like.

EARS AND NECK

Many women find their ears one of the most sensitive spots on their bodies. Encourage your hubby to explore—to kiss, to nibble, to blow gently. And necks invite passionate kisses.

HANDS AND FEET

Fingers and toes tend to like being sucked. When you're newly married, many women feel a bit shy and think they're smelly, so wash beforehand and you won't need to have these qualms.

LEGS, ARMS, AND BACKS

Most women love massage. The more he rubs your back, or strokes your legs or your arms, the more other areas of your body will call out for attention. Our bodies crave touch all over, and when you're naked and your husband touches you in places other than the typical erogenous zones, the teasing can be delicious. By not touching you between your legs right away, for instance, he'll make you more aware of how much that part of your body yearns to be touched. So pass him some massage oil and give him permission to tease you.

Once you've warmed up and you start to feel tingling in your erogenous zones, those areas will likely want to be touched too. (You're moving from excited to aroused.) So now it's time for him to touch you more sexually.

BREASTS

If you aren't well-endowed, don't worry that being diminutive in the bra department means your breasts won't appreciate some attention. Size bears no relation to sensitivity, something for which I am eternally grateful.

Remember how I mentioned that men often like to be stroked and squeezed with pressure, while women like to be touched more gently? This is especially true around the nipple area. A guy's approach can often be too rough. Show him the right pressure (you don't even have to use words if you're shy, just take his hand). When you become aroused, your nipples will become erect and hard, similar to when you're cold. When you're excited, you can often handle (and even yearn for) more direct pressure. So while you may prefer that he starts out gently, you may not mind something firmer later. This applies to his mouth too: a gentle lick may work at first, but later you may want something more. Let him know, even if it means murmuring when he's doing something delicious!

Some women, though, just find any nipple stimulation a turn off. If that's you, that's okay! Just move on to other parts of your body.

CLITORIS

The clitoris has no purpose in the body except arousal. Men don't have any bits of anatomy that are meant only to make them feel good, but God made women with this little knob of flesh that has only one purpose: to make us fly when we're with our husbands. God wants you to have a good time. He wants you to love sex! Cool, isn't it?

It's not surprising, then, that the most important erogenous zone in us girls is the clitoris, the knob of flesh between the two outer lips (labia majora), right in front of the opening for the vagina. Almost button-like, it protrudes a bit from your body. It's the most sensitive part of you, containing eight thousand nerve endings—as many as the penis, even though the clitoris is much smaller. It's a little bundle of intense pleasure.

Because it's so sensitive, your husband may be too rough initially because he doesn't know how to touch it (and perhaps you don't either). He may go too far to the right or the left.

Think of your vulva like a clock, with 12:00 being right above your clitoris, and 6:00 being the bottom opening of your vagina, pointing toward the anus. The clitoris usually enjoys being touched from the direction of 12:00, not from the direction of 6:00 (as in, go down, don't go up). That's because between the clitoris and the vagina is the urethra, the hole where urine comes out. And that feels distinctly unsexy if it's stimulated. If he rubs from there upward to try to find the clitoris, it can feel off-putting. So help him approach from the top.

When you're getting warmed up, often circles or figure eights or even going back and forth feels good. Later on, you may like it just being pressed. The key is communication. If it feels good, tell him. If it's too much or too rough or not exactly the right spot, reposition his hand. Men often have a hard time figuring out right where the clitoris is, and you can act as his tour guide.

VAGINA

Though the clitoris is the most sensitive area on a woman's body, guys often assume it's the vagina, since that's where the "main event" happens. The vagina is one of those areas that women either love to have touched and probed or hate to have touched and probed. At one church event where I gave my signature Girl Talk about sex and marriage, I received this question during our Q&A: "Why does my husband always approach my vagina like he's digging for gold?" I didn't have a good answer for her, but many women have told me similar stories. Sometimes a guy assumes that what feels best for a woman is to have his fingers explore inside her.

Again, some women like this, and some don't. Sometimes what women like is the feeling of being "full," so more fingers may be better than fewer. Others like him to stimulate her as if he's making a "come here" sign with his forefinger, reaching up the front wall of her vagina. It's the front wall, where the clitoral roots extend, that is often the most sensitive. And some women don't like this type of stimulation at all. It doesn't matter what group you're in. You have to figure out what *your* body likes and find a way to tell him, even if it means moaning when he does something rapturous.

When and if you want him to explore inside you, some women swear by the "G-spot," a quarter-sized area between one and three inches inside the vagina on the front wall (the wall closest to your stomach, not your back). Rubbing there with the penis or the fingers is the easiest way for some women to experience orgasm. But if you can't find the G-spot, that's okay! Just have fun hunting. As one commenter said, "I don't consciously set out to locate it every single time. However, each time I do, it's heavenly!"

What if you've tried some of these ideas and nothing happens? Listen to Natalie's story:

> When I didn't orgasm for the first 7 years of our relationship, even he came to the conclusion that my body must just be broken. In the early days, he tried to stimulate my clitoris or find the G-spot, but he was very rough and didn't use lube and we were both too young and inexperienced to know any better. Mind you, my husband is an extremely kind, empathetic, caring man and always has been . . . which is also why it baffled me so much that we had such awful, physical-exchange-like sex for nearly a decade! But when I didn't orgasm after a month of him trying to figure out my body when we were both 19, he and I both concluded that it must be my body was broken, not that he still had more work to do to figure me out or that I had more work to do in uncovering and embracing my sexual side. I'm sure there are many good men out there like my husband who are just rather clueless about sex and think trying new things will result in instant results.

Sisters, sex is supposed to feel awesome. If you take your time, pay attention to your body, and tell him when something feels great, then you should expect some fireworks! But if you're like Natalie, and your husband's been rubbing, probing, and licking, but nothing's sizzling, then take heart—this next chapter is specifically for you.

CHAPTER 4

Reaching for the Stars

I was sixteen years old, sitting in one of the back pews at a large church in Toronto at a youth conference, flanked on either side by two guys that I sort of liked (I was trying to decide which one I should start obsessing about). As all youth conferences do, the conversation turned to sex, and we all perked up. But then the speaker said something that made me want to slide out of my pew and crawl underneath it.

He talked about the clitoris.

He talked about how God gave the clitoris to women even though it has no other purpose than sexual pleasure.

He talked about how sex was for women just as much as for men but that messing around with sex too early could . . . well, to be honest, I don't have a clue what he said after that. I only remember the clitoris part.

Why is it that we consider female pleasure mortifying? Maybe you don't (your mama raised you right!), but for many, the mere mention of the clitoris seems more personal than hearing the word *penis*. It seems more forbidden, more secret, more hidden.

Perhaps that makes sense because the clitoris *is* more hidden than the penis. Maybe that's why we tend to have such a difficult time finding it. In the last chapter, we explored what the sexual response cycle looks like and how men and women tend to experience arousal and pleasure. For some of you, that's all the information you need. But many women struggle with reaching orgasm. In fact, it's much easier for most men than for most women. In our surveys of almost twenty-five thousand Christian men and women, we found that our orgasm rates are quite different. Just over 95 percent of Christian men report reaching orgasm "almost always or always" during sex, compared with just under 49 percent of women. That's roughly a forty-seven-point orgasm gap.[1]

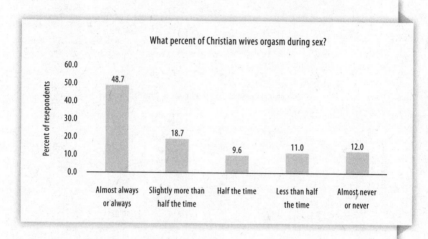

Some of you are looking at that chart, and you're not in the 49 percent. You're not experiencing anything near orgasm, and you're despairing, wondering if it will ever be possible. But take heart! My survey found that the best years for sex in marriage are not the honeymoon years or even the first decade—they're years sixteen through twenty.[2] After that amount of time, you're comfortable with each other, babies are grown up and you're getting a full night's sleep again, and you're able to tell him what you like. Many women who are in that 49 percent category were once in the 12 percent. But they figured it out.

And the best age for orgasm isn't the late teens or twenties—it's the forties![3]

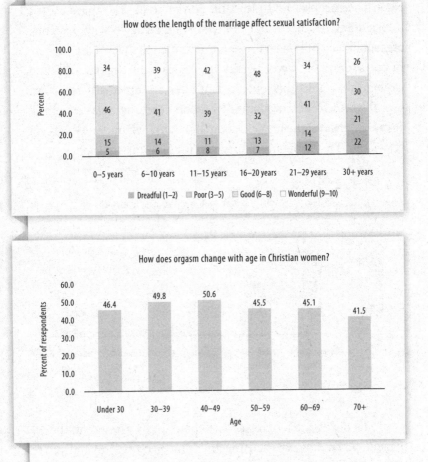

How does the length of the marriage affect sexual satisfaction?

Dreadful (1–2)   Poor (3–5)   Good (6–8)   Wonderful (9–10)

How does orgasm change with age in Christian women?

But I know that achieving orgasm can be difficult, so I want to dedicate a whole chapter to it. Let's start by spending a little more time on the clitoris because it tells us some key things about what God meant for sex.

The Clitoris Means That God Wants You to Feel Pleasure

Like the youth speaker told me back when I still permed my hair, God intended for women to feel pleasure. Sex is not mostly for men, with women's pleasure as an afterthought. Sex is something specifically designed to make women feel good—really good! If that's God's design, then why is it often so elusive? Here's my theory: our definition of sex is too narrow.

When we get married, many of us rejoice because we can finally "have sex." And what we mean by "have sex" tends to be "have intercourse." Now, intercourse is an important part of a couple's sexual life. But defining sex as merely intercourse can leave your experience out of the story. If sex is simply him putting his penis into your vagina and moving around until he climaxes (sorry for being crass, but I want to be clear here!), then you could be lying there making a grocery list in your head, you could be lying there upset and feeling used, you could even be in pain, and it would still count as "having sex."

We know that's not what God meant for sex. We've looked at how sex is supposed to be mutual and intimate and pleasurable for both, and so, to God, your pleasure matters. Your experience matters. But because we're so focused on intercourse, we often rush to have intercourse on our honeymoon, skipping steps in the sexual response cycle. He feels amazing, while you may not feel much of anything. You may even wonder, "Is that it?"

Slowly but surely, as weeks go by, months go by, even *years* go by, just like Natalie, you worry that you're broken. He feels great all the time. Maybe sex isn't for you.

I want to assure you, whether you're about to get married and you're scared or excited, whether you've just gotten married and you're a little bewildered, or whether you've been married for

> **You are not broken.**

years and you've almost given up hope: *you are not broken*. Your clitoris isn't broken. Your vagina isn't broken. Your body isn't broken!

It may be that you and your husband have never learned the lessons that God wanted you to learn about how he made the clitoris.

If sex is going to feel good, you need to accept the way God made your body and work *with* your body. He made you this way for a reason. And that reason should give you a clue about what he wants *for* you in the bedroom.

You Were Meant to Be the Center of Attention

How did you feel about walking down the aisle on your wedding day? Maybe for you, this was the moment you'd been waiting for your whole life: the day that you could be the center of attention as you married the man you loved more than life itself. Or maybe that wasn't your attitude at all. Maybe instead this was the day you'd marry the man you loved more than life itself, even if you *had* to be the center of attention. Some women love having every eye on them; and some women feel awkward. Not everyone revels in being in the limelight.

We all have some scenarios where being the center of attention is more comfortable than in others. But even if it is uncomfortable for you right now, you were meant to be the center of attention in the bedroom at times, and he was meant to fuss over you.

Many women spend their lives looking after everyone else and thinking of other people first. Whether it's our parents, our friends, our kids, even our coworkers, our mental and emotional energy is spent for other people's well-being.

But God made women's bodies so that to feel good, we have to do two things: we have to stop thinking about everyone else and concentrate on what we are feeling, and we have to let someone else serve us. It's like God's gift to us, telling us, *Let someone else take care of you for a while.* It's not selfish to want foreplay. It's not selfish for him to have to stimulate you directly in order for you to feel good. This is the way God made you!

God did not place the clitoris up inside the vagina so that it would receive maximum stimulation from intercourse (when your husband is also experiencing maximum stimulation). No, he placed it in front of the vagina so that you need more direct stimulation from your husband in some way. *The clitoris means that the pleasure you're supposed to feel will come mostly from your husband paying attention to your body in ways that don't necessarily directly stimulate him.* The clitoris tells us that for you to feel good, your husband needs to spend some time pleasuring you. God meant for you to be the center of attention!

You Do Not Take Too Long

On average, women take about fourteen minutes to reach orgasm once they are aroused (and up to twenty minutes or so is not atypical). The average man takes only five minutes. We take a long time!

Or do we? After all, if the average man took forty-five minutes, then we'd think we were rockets. We think we take a long time because *compared to men* we do. But again, this is God's design for our bodies. And maybe God created women to take longer than men so that men would have to be unselfish and serve us and so that we would learn to allow them to serve us.

Your Pleasure Should Not Be an Afterthought

Of the women in our survey who could reach orgasm, only 39 percent could do so through intercourse alone. The others needed a lot of foreplay, and many could do so in other ways but not through intercourse. *And there is nothing wrong with that* Nobody gets a special badge for orgasming through intercourse. Sure, it's fun, but orgasm itself is fun, and how you get there doesn't really matter.

Too often a woman will use her husband's experience as a measuring stick and then fear she's inferior and less sexual. *He feels good easily; there must be something wrong with me. He only needs intercourse; it's selfish of me to want too much of something else. He's really fast; he must enjoy sex more and do it better.* No! He's a man, and you're a woman, and you have different body parts that were designed to work in different ways. And God is clear that your pleasure is as important as your husband's, and we know that because of the clitoris.

There. Now we've come full circle (which is kind of funny considering we're talking about the clitoris), but let's see how understanding why God made the clitoris like he did plays out when it comes to orgasm.

Your Orgasm Matters Just as Much as His Does

When we conducted our survey of twenty thousand women last year, we found a multitude of reasons why women have trouble reaching orgasm. But one stood out more than any other: lack of foreplay.

We asked both men and women, "Do you think you do enough foreplay?" When women frequently orgasm, men overwhelmingly say they do—and women tend to agree (though not in quite as high numbers; seems like many women would like more foreplay regardless!). But when women don't frequently orgasm? Men *still* say they do enough foreplay—and so do the majority of women. That makes me wonder, "Enough for what?" Let's say I decided I needed to get

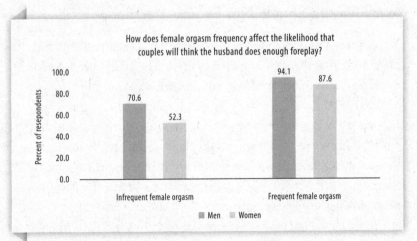

How does female orgasm frequency affect the likelihood that couples will think the husband does enough foreplay?

a part-time job so I would have enough money to buy a small car. How would I judge when I had earned "enough"? Likely when I had enough money in my savings account to match the sticker price on the car, right? So why do women in such large numbers think their husbands have done enough even when they don't reach orgasm?

One woman explained it like this:

I'm worried that I have subconsciously taught myself not to experience any pleasure during intercourse because I usually don't get even mildly aroused until my husband is almost done. I've thought about this a fair bit, and I think it's because I know that stopping at a bit of arousal every time, and not getting to orgasm, leaves me feeling so unsatisfied. I suppose I've convinced myself that it's more satisfying to watch him have fun than it is to start having fun myself, but then not finish. Yes, we have tried to focus on me after he's climaxed, but then I always feel bad because he's obviously spent, and then my "feeling bad" stops it from happening anyways . . . so subconsciously I go back to square one: "Why bother allowing myself to get turned on in the first place?"

We feel like it's selfish to want more. We figure we don't work right. But, my sisters, sex will never feel good until you decide that you're worth it. It is okay to want your husband to pay attention to your pleasure.

Imagine a world where what women need in order to feel loved is to go out to eat at a restaurant at least once a week, where they talk and enjoy a delicious meal. This is the pinnacle of marriage to her.

Picture a couple, Tracey and Doug, who tries to live by this. One Tuesday night our intrepid couple heads to a restaurant. They order appetizers, a main course, and a dessert.

The waitress arrives with Tracey's appetizer—a steaming bowl of cheese and broccoli soup. Tracey finishes it and declares it delicious. But nothing comes for Doug. Then Tracey's steak arrives. Doug's still wondering where his appetizer is, but Tracey starts slathering the butter and sour cream onto the baked potato and takes a bite of the steak with peppercorn sauce and asparagus. She declares it scrumptious.

Now Tracey is finished with her steak, and the waitress heads toward the couple again. In front of Tracey she places a steaming, luscious molten lava cake. Tracey squeals in delight as she scoops some out. Just as she's down to the last few spoonfuls, the waitress finally arrives with Doug's chicken wing appetizer. Doug's ecstatic, and he digs in, eating one quickly, and then another. But before he can get to his third one, Tracey stands up, ready to go home. "Dinner was amazing," she declares as she heads for the door. He follows behind her, glancing at the uneaten chicken wings still on his plate, while Tracey says, "I love doing this with you!"

Imagine that Doug and Tracey faithfully do this every week for ten years. How do you think Doug will feel about eating at restaurants?

It's easy to have sympathy for Doug in that situation. It's all so unfair!

What I'd ask you to do now is have sympathy for yourself too. It is not unfair to want pleasure for yourself. It is not selfish to need foreplay. You are not broken if intercourse alone doesn't bring you to orgasm. Sex is as much for you as it is for him, and it's important that your sex life reflect that. Often one of the big reasons we don't reach orgasm is that we feel guilty or selfish if we want anything extra, or we feel like sex isn't primarily for us anyway. Getting through these mental roadblocks is the first big step toward great sex![4]

Orgasm Means Letting Go—And Not Worrying So Much

Even if you decide your pleasure is worth it, there's another mental roadblock that can come up. You can put so much pressure on yourself that you make orgasm even more elusive. Movies may paint orgasm as the most natural thing in the world, but just because it's natural doesn't mean it's second nature. Again, this doesn't mean you're not sexual. God created you so that you would have to communicate and work together to achieve great sex, which encourages you to work on emotional connection too. It all feeds each other! But *working* toward orgasm can be an obstacle in itself. If you're nervous about attaining orgasm, you're less likely to get there.

You need to feel relaxed, comfortable, and cherished before you can even become aroused. And then, once you're aroused, you need to be even more relaxed before you can climax. At its most basic, an orgasm involves a woman losing control and surrendering. You can't do that if you're still holding back, and worrying about whether you're going to get there is a big part of holding back. So you have to learn to relax. That's much easier to do if you have this attitude: *This will happen eventually. So let's try for it, but let's not get all worked up about it. Let's just enjoy ourselves and see what happens!* That being said, there's nothing wrong with trying to reach for the sky.

Sometimes our tension goes even deeper. An orgasm is the ultimate in letting go: you can't climax if you overanalyze everything. You have to let your body be swept away. That can be difficult for some women because it means letting go of control. Many of us like our lives orderly, clean, and predictable. One reason we're not always fond of our bodies is because they can be smelly and messy and awkward. Sex, then, can seem distasteful at best, if not downright wrong. Letting go, being vulnerable, and being messy can all seem unsettling.

As much as we may think that being orderly is next to being godly, God is the one who designed sex to be messy! He doesn't want us to feel in control, because we're not supposed to be in control—he is. And so perhaps it's only natural that in the most intimate moments, we're not supposed to be clean and tame and sterile. Throw your head back and go with it. If that's a little intimidating, take some deep breaths and get comfortable with each other's bodies until you can value them just as they were made. Don't be afraid to tell your husband if you're struggling and need to slow down while you make love. The more time he gives you, the better it will turn out for both of you.

Now let's move on to practical steps to rev up arousal.

Let's Bridge the Gap!

Use Your Brain

Shortly after we were married, my husband, who never gets sick, developed a rash all over and a fever of 102. After letting him sleep for a bit, I tiptoed to the bedroom and opened the door to check on him. "Is there anything I can do for you?" I asked sympathetically. Immediately his bloodshot eyes grew wider as he replied, smirking, "Well, since you mentioned it . . ." In my newlywed state, I assumed that he was sick, in more ways than one.

While many men are focused on the body and become aroused easily and stay aroused easily, many of us women find that far trickier. Sex is often more in our heads than it is between our legs. And that's why a fever of 102 would be a big turnoff. If we can't concentrate on what's going on, we won't become aroused.

Often I'll be having a fun time with Keith, when out of the blue I think, "Is there milk in the fridge for cereal in the morning?" I didn't mean to think about milk. The thought just wandered in there. But once it's in my head, it's hard to banish it. "Well, if there's no milk, what else can we have for breakfast? And when am I going to have a chance to buy some? Can I go before lunch? I wonder what else I should pick up." My poor husband, who thought he was doing so well, knows he has lost me. And it's all because of a grocery item.

There's a positive side and a negative side to sex being in our heads. The negative is that we are easily distracted, and we have to work hard on keeping our mind focused on what we want our bodies

What is the effect of women's arousal during sex on a couple's marital and sexual satisfaction? (How many times more or less likely are they to experience the following?)	
I frequently orgasm during sex	17.3
I am satisfied with the amount of closeness I share with my husband during sex	11.1
I am comfortable talking to my husband about what feels good sexually and what I want sexually	6.6
I feel that my husband considers my needs, desires, and wants in our marriage as much as he does his own	3.8
I am satisfied with the amount of housework my husband does	2.6
I am confident my husband is not tempted by other women	2.3
I often feel uncomfortable about how my husband looks at other women when we are in public	-3
When we have conflict, I don't feel like my husband really hears me	-3.3

to respond to. But the positive is that we do have some control. I have heard it said that men are like microwaves and women are like slow cookers, and I don't think it's only because men are done fast. It's supposed to be because men heat up quickly, while women take more time. But calling women slow cookers implies that we will, eventually, heat up. But there's no guarantee. It all depends on our heads.

In general, women become aroused *when we allow ourselves to be*. Letting our guard down makes us more vulnerable during sex because we need to willingly open ourselves up to enjoy it. We need to let him in, not only physically but emotionally as well. Great sex isn't about lying back and assuming that when he does things just right, it will feel good. It's throwing yourself into the process. It's deciding to let yourself become aroused. It's deciding to pay attention.

Practice Listening to Your Body

Many of us grow up disconnected from our bodies. To think about your body is to be reminded that you're not good enough. You haven't exercised lately. You ate a whole bag of chips last night. You had ice cream for breakfast. When I grew up, a teenager would feel mortified if her bra strap showed. I'm grateful that now camisoles and bra straps can be fashion statements.

But the female body has often been seen as bad. It's not surprising that many of us go through life trying not to feel anything below our necks because we don't want to be reminded—reminded of something that causes shame, reminded that we don't like our bodies, reminded that we feel inadequate.

But for great sex, you have to let yourself *feel*. If you find this a challenge, try some of these exercises.

STRETCHING OR YOGA

Start the day with a ten-minute stretching or yoga routine because stretching allows you to feel different parts of your body in a nonsexual way. A quick perusal of YouTube offers a plethora of possibilities. Stretch more, and you learn to lean into the stretch, adjusting so that it feels even better. You listen and respond to what your body tells you to do.

MASSAGE

Back massage is another great way to learn what wants to be touched. Have your husband grab some massage oil and begin rubbing with long strokes (again, YouTube videos give some massage tips). As he rubs, you'll feel what areas need some special touch. Direct him to those areas and lean in.

NOW LET'S GET SEXY!

Sexual touch is similar. You feel your body being touched, and then you listen to what parts of your body want more. When something starts calling out for attention, you may also realize that it wants *different*—more intense, faster, even a little to the left! It's all about valuing your own body's responses rather than forcing or expecting your body to respond "like it should." Every time you say "should" or "you're supposed to" to your body, stop, back up, and put yourself in a time-out so you can repeat, "I am beautifully and wonderfully made, and my body is just fine!"

Great sex isn't found by following a blueprint. Reducing sex to a series of tick boxes like some preflight checklist is the opposite of great sex. "Remove clothing. *Check*. Clitoral stimulation commencing. *Check*." That's not sexy at all. If, instead of moving through steps at your own pace, you obediently follow some protocol, you're likely to feel like a science experiment or a zoo exhibit. One newlywed woman explained it like this:

> I'm just starting to figure out my body, and I know that I can reach orgasm now through touching myself. I want my husband to be able to help me as well, but we'll have sex, and then he'll be down between my legs, rubbing randomly, looking at my face to see if it's having any effect, with this expression going between me being a science experiment and him being a sad puppy. Half the time I just push him away and tell him, "It's okay, we can just go to sleep."

Sad puppies are not sexy. Impersonal scientists are not sexy. Looking at the bedside clock to see how long he's been at it is not sexy. These reactions take you out of the moment and make you worry about what he's feeling or that you're somehow inadequate.

Instead, give yourself permission to pay attention to what wants to be touched, and to communicate that to your husband so that you can work through the arousal steps *as your body wants to*.

As your body works through the sexual response cycle, what your body wants may change. If your husband tries to touch your nipples, for instance, let alone pinch or squeeze them when you're not aroused, it might hurt, and you might think, "Stop that!" If you want him to stop, say it out loud. Sometimes we don't speak up because we think we're supposed to like something, but if you don't like it, say so! Remember this simple truth: *if you put up with something you don't really like, your husband will probably do it for the next twenty years*. If you don't like it today, you're not likely to want it in several decades either. So do future you a favor and say, "Not quite like that."

> Do future you a favor and say, "Not quite like that."

But it may not be that you don't like your nipples being touched. It may simply be that *unaroused* you—or only slightly excited you—doesn't like her nipples being touched. Once you're almost at orgasm, you may quite enjoy it. Or you may not and find something else even better. Your body is your own.

That's why arousal and orgasm can't be paint-by-number. It's not that certain techniques or actions will necessarily feel good to you. It's that they may feel good when your body is ready.

And while you listen, don't forget to keep kissing! One large study of over fifty thousand adults found that women were more likely to have reached orgasm in their last sexual encounter if it included deep kissing, even more than if it included intercourse.[5] Expressing love during sex is key to women's sexual response.

TELL HIM WHAT YOU WANT

He has different body parts than you do, and his body responds differently than yours does, so he isn't going to know what to do unless you tell him! That's why, even if it's awkward, it's best to speak up about what parts of you want to be touched.

But what if you don't know how to describe what you want? And if you've never said words like *vagina* or *clitoris*, doing so may feel awkward. But chances are you can say "a little to the left" or "just like that" or "faster, please." And you can guide his hand. You can even make a game out of helping you each learn to communicate better about what feels good.

Practice giving instructions that have nothing to do with sex! Describe the following:

a. a particular nonerogenous spot on your body that you want him to touch (say, two inches down on your left shoulder blade) and

b. exactly how you want it touched (rubbed slowly in circles, rubbed fast, what level of pressure, and so on).

Because this practice has nothing to do with sex, there's no need to feel self-conscious. You know when you want him to massage a particular place and he keeps going everywhere but that place? Think of this as a similar game. How can you get him to touch exactly the right place, and describe exactly what motion you want? Then practice on a different body part, or have him give you instructions.

HAVE A HARD TIME GIVING DIRECTIONS? PLAY THE OPTOMETRIST GAME!

When you take an eye test, the optometrist has you look through a bulky machine while giving you options: "Which is better? A or B?" Once you answer "B," then they compare B and C. Do the same thing with sex! Have your husband rub your clitoris two different ways, then tell him which is better. Then have him change it up again. Or have him stroke your breasts two different ways. Do you like to be kissed behind your knees or on your toes? Choosing between two options may be easier than answering, "What do you want me to do now?" Plus, it can be more fun!

Heading for Orgasm

If you're worried about not reaching orgasm or feeling pressure to reach it, start your night together with a bath, a massage, or something that helps you relax. Spend some time talking. Make sure you feel loved, cherished, and accepted before you move on. Start the night remembering that sex isn't a pass-or-fail test; it is a chance for both of you to feel close.

Now, once you start the sexy stuff, first aim for orgasm in ways other than intercourse. It's usually easier to reach climax from your husband stimulating your clitoris either manually or orally (with his fingers or his mouth) than it is through intercourse. That doesn't mean you'll never experience an orgasm when he's inside you; it simply means that it sometimes takes time to perfect the technique. The more you learn to experience an orgasm another way, the easier it can be to have an orgasm through intercourse. You'll then know what feels good, and you'll be far more aware of the changes your body is going through and your various arousal levels.

So let me say it again: *you do not have to reach orgasm through intercourse on your wedding night, or even on your honeymoon* (and we have a whole appendix on how to have an amazing honeymoon). Many women take a few years of marriage to accomplish this feat. It's a great goal to reach orgasm some other way (such as through manual stimulation), but if you're too tense, don't rush it. Do what seems fun to you. Learn to relax while being naked together and touching each other.

Once you're able to reach orgasm with oral or manual stimulation, you'll likely want to see if you can ride that momentum to reach orgasm during intercourse. One of the challenges of this is that the transition from foreplay to intercourse often causes your arousal to plummet. Before, you were getting direct stimulation; now you may get less, and that can bring the sexual response cycle to a halt. But it doesn't have to, and here are some tips to help you keep going.

Don't Start Intercourse Until You're Almost There

Does orgasm through intercourse still seem out of reach? Let's help get you there! Work first at identifying your arousal levels. Let him bring you to orgasm in other ways, but as he does so, pay attention to how aroused you feel, on a scale of one to ten.

Intermittently, have him stop and ask you to rate your arousal level. Notice how you're breathing, how wet you are, and how much you want him to keep going. Recognize the difference, for instance, between a seven and a four. Then note the difference between a nine and a seven. Think of nine as the stage where it wouldn't take much to put you over the edge—that point where if he were to stop, you'd grab him and desperately beg him to keep going. Just a little touch and you'll be there. By this point, your clitoris will have retracted so it's flat against the body, so any "pressing" will feel exciting. If you transition to intercourse once you're at this level, you can still maintain arousal because all you need is that pressure from his thrusting to send you over the edge.

Once you've had a few sessions of this fun and you're both familiar with what a nine is, have him stimulate you until you reach nine, and then start intercourse. Hopefully you'll reach orgasm quickly. Once this is easy for you, try to do the same thing starting at arousal level eight, and then at seven. The more attention you pay to your body's cues, the easier it will be for you to let go.

Get the Right Angle

Remember that clitoral stimulation is what brings a woman to orgasm even during intercourse, so make sure you're at an angle where your clitoris receives stimulation. One simple trick is to tilt your pelvis up when you're in the missionary position (you on bottom, him on top). When your hips are tilted up at a forty-five-degree angle and he's entering you at the same angle, his pelvic bone will hit your clitoris every time he thrusts.

Some women place a pillow under their rump, but that doesn't work as well because the act of physically tilting your pelvis yourself puts some pressure on the clitoris already (seriously, just try it; tilt your pelvis forward by tensing the muscles in your bum, and you'll feel your clitoris getting squeezed). Merely sticking a pillow under you doesn't engage the muscles. But do both in combination and you'll likely have a winner!

Other women find it easier to make sure the clitoris gets enough pressure by making love while she is on top. Move your body up and down around his penis, and each time you come down, aim so that your clitoris falls into contact with his pelvis.

When orgasm does occur during intercourse, it can feel slightly different from a clitoral orgasm, as if the pleasure centers in a different area. It's less focused on one part of your body and more focused on the whole genital area, or even deeper inside the body. A clitoral orgasm is often more intense, and you're frequently very sensitive afterward, far more so than with a vaginal one. But perhaps *intense* isn't the right word. If you relax during the orgasm and just experience it, rather than feeling that you're "done," you may find that it can last a long time. With practice you can even feel secondary and tertiary waves afterward. But orgasm is the one thing you will never reach if you're worried about it.

Exercises to Increase Stimulation

The more that you can control how hard you squeeze when he's inside you, the more stimulation you can get from intercourse. And, hey, you can exercise those muscles!

HOW TO DO KEGEL EXERCISES

Kegel exercises strengthen your muscles and increase sensitivity—plus they provide a host of other benefits, such as preparing you for childbirth, stopping urinary incontinence, and more. Here's how you do them:

1. Identify the muscles. When you're peeing, stop the flow midstream. The muscles that you used to do this are the same muscles you squeeze and relax during a Kegel.[6]
2. Squeeze and relax. The Mayo Clinic suggests imagining that you're sitting on a marble, and then tightening the pelvic muscles as if you're lifting that marble. Squeeze for three seconds and then relax for a count of three.
3. Keep everything else relaxed. Don't tighten the muscles in your abdomen, thighs, or bum. Isolate the pelvic floor.
4. Breathe!
5. Repeat this three times a day, with five repetitions each time.

Expanding Your Repertoire

Once you figure out how to orgasm, or how to do so more often, you'll likely wonder, "How can we have even more fun?" That's often when couples try a new sex position manual or book. But trying new positions with a diagram can feel awkward. You're going all hot and heavy and then you have to stop, pull out the diagram, and readjust. And it can be hard to focus when sex is more like a game of Twister than an intimate experience with your husband.

Let's make this easier. Most positions fall into one of four categories:

1. Face to face, man on top
2. Face to face, woman on top
3. Man facing her back, man on top
4. Man facing her back, woman on top

The man-on-top, woman-on-bottom position (otherwise known as the missionary position) is the most common go-to position. You can also look each other in the eyes, which is intimate.

A few tips to make this one as comfortable as possible: tilt your pelvis. Don't use a pillow under your head because that can raise the top of your body and distort the angle where you need it to be just right. Make sure that he has something to anchor his feet on, since it's hard to thrust (move back and forth) without some kind of leverage. If he can anchor his feet, it's easier for him to take some of the weight off you too. If there's a big weight discrepancy between the two of you, have him put some weight onto his forearms so you don't feel like you're being suffocated. Try it, and if you can't breathe, laugh about it, shove him up, and get the position the way you want it. Do this early in your marriage because you want to set the stage for finding out what feels good. You don't want to be uncomfortable for a year without saying anything and then tell him it's been unpleasant all along.

Another alternative is the woman-on-top, man-on-bottom position. This one usually involves him lying down and you straddling him while sitting up. This position is intense because you can still look in his eyes, and he often likes it because he gets a good view of you bouncing around (he can also touch your breasts more easily). If he's a lot heavier than you, this can also be more comfortable for you. When you're beginning your sex life together, being on top can also be less stressful because you can take control. You're the one who decides how deep to go, so if you feel tender or you're still getting used to penetration, you can experiment a bit and make sure to do what feels good. Again, because you're the one on top, you can also arrange for the clitoris to come into contact with his pelvic bone more easily and can sometimes control your own pleasure a little more. This was the only comfortable position for one new bride:

I wish I had known the position that "worked" was me on top. We tried the "missionary" position but couldn't get penetration because that was too uncomfortable for me. We actually fell asleep before successfully having sex and then woke up sometime later and were able to figure it out better. I know my husband was disappointed at first when he thought it wouldn't work, but then later . . . he definitely wasn't!

Another popular position is the "rear entry" position, where the woman typically kneels on all fours, and he kneels behind her and penetrates from behind. (I'm not talking about anal sex here; he's still entering the vagina.) Many men are rather eager to try this one because they feel powerful, and it is awfully intense for them. But some people shy away from it because it doesn't seem as intimate. It's your call (more on that in chapter 8).

However, this position can be uncomfortable when you are new to sex because the angle is different and tends to feel quite a bit tighter. If you experience pain the first time you make love, then trying this right away is not a good idea. It's better to save the more adventurous stuff for later in your marriage.

Nevertheless, if you want to give it a shot, the benefits are that he can easily put a hand, or a finger, on your clitoris while you make love, and thus stimulate you that way while you're having intercourse. Guide him in this, or he may be too rough. Some women also find that this position is the best one for stimulating the G-spot.

Of course, our bodies fit together in any number of ways, and once you're comfortable, experiment all you want. You don't need a long list of positions as much as you need an imagination! If you find a new way his penis can fit inside you, go with it. Sometimes varying what you do with your legs can make a position feel different too. Wrapping your legs around his torso in the missionary position, for instance, lets him go deeper. Putting your legs over his shoulders takes some flexibility but lets him feel like he's going even farther. So try intercourse sitting or with him standing or with your legs up or down, and it will feel different each time. (Just never let his penis bear your weight. It can break, and that requires a trip to the emergency room!) By changing whether you're sitting in a chair or lying on a bed, you'll also vary the angle at which he enters you, even if he's the one on the bottom both times. Just don't pressure yourself to do anything you're not ready for. You have a lifetime to get this right, and if it doesn't click on the first try, laugh about it. It's trial and error for at least the first few years with most couples anyway. But that trial-and-error period will be shortened if you become comfortable with telling him what feels good.

Enjoy the Journey

Even with all these pointers, orgasm may not come instantaneously. Please don't see sex as a pass-or-fail test or feel like you're not doing it right; let yourself enjoy it, and keep aiming for the stars! Remember: orgasm is usually easier in ways other than intercourse. Make sure each sexual encounter has something in it for both of you, even if it's a massage first for you. And keep trying because *you are not broken.*

What makes sex amazing isn't just orgasms anyway. It's so much more than that. So let's turn to the next aspect of intimacy that God designed us for.

Spiritual Intimacy

CHAPTER 5

Learning to Make Love, Not Just Have Sex

On September 4, 1996, the phone rang at 1:30 in the morning. I was out of bed like a rocket because I knew what that meant. Earlier that evening we had said good night to our baby boy, lying in the pediatric intensive care unit at the Hospital for Sick Children in Toronto. Four days had elapsed since his open-heart surgery, and that day had not been a good one. But by the time we had left his bedside on September 3, he appeared to have turned the corner, and the danger seemed to have passed.

As soon as that phone rang, I knew that our relief was to be short-lived. The nurse on the other end of the line told me we had better come fast.

An hour later that same nurse brought out the body of our son and laid him in my arms.

We left the hospital at 3:30 a.m. and trudged the few blocks home. We climbed back into bed and didn't know what to do. We couldn't plan the funeral yet; it was the middle of the night. We couldn't go back to sleep. We were in shock. And so we held each other and kissed each other until the kissing turned into something more.

It was not that we were physically aroused. Rather, we were so grieved and needed to be close to the only other individual on this earth who shared our pain. We needed to touch each other.

We hope you never have the need to make love in a moment of overwhelming grief, but at the same time, it was a precious experience for us because we both felt how sex was something so much deeper than physical pleasure. It was the joining of everything we were, the compulsive need to be united. A marriage is not complete if the couple has sex only for physical release; they also need the extraordinary spiritual closeness that sex was designed for.

Sex Is More Than Physical

In this book we describe the three aspects of great sex: learning how everything works physically, experiencing the deep connection that comes through making love, and creating a great friendship that fuels passion. It's that deep connection that we turn to in this chapter and the next. But that deep connection is often the hardest because it's the most fragile. It depends on being able both to express and feel love through sex. And that expressing and feeling can be challenging.

Let's first look at the barriers some women have in experiencing that connection during sex and then discover the common outcome—and common solution—to these problems.

Problem #1: Seeing Sex as Something Dirty or Shameful

Did you grow up feeling like sex was shameful? Maybe your mom swatted your hands away if they ever strayed near your genitals, or maybe she didn't tell you the proper words for your body parts. Or perhaps it's not the messages about sex you received growing up; it's the messages about sex you receive now. Instead of sex feeling like a deep knowing, it feels like something degrading. Sex is painted as a man's basic need, and you feel used. *You have to have sex or he'll watch* porn. *You need to have sex or he'll lust. You need to give him sexual release every few days or he won't feel loved.* It feels as if you need to give your body to satisfy him but that you're missing from the equation. Sex doesn't feel like an intimate knowing, but rather a one-sided obligation. In our book *The Great Sex Rescue* we showed how these messages harm women's sexuality, aren't biblical, and often aren't even believed by husbands themselves. In fact, 71 percent of men told us they don't believe they need their wives to have sex to prevent their porn use, and 77 percent don't believe their wives owe them sex when they want it, even though 43 percent of women report being taught this message. When women believe that sex is an obligation, sex can feel threatening rather than uniting. (If your husband is in the 29 percent of men who think you are what is standing between him and porn, or the 23 percent of men who think you do owe him sex, please seek help from a licensed counselor because these are red flags for abuse. Sex should feel like he is honoring and cherishing you, not that he is objectifying you and using you.)

What is the effect of a husband believing that sex prevents porn use on a couple's marital and sexual satisfaction? (How many times more or less likely are they to experience the following?)	
I feel that my wife considers my needs, desires, and wants in our marriage as much as she does her own	-2.1
I am satisfied with the amount of enthusiasm my wife shows in the bedroom	-2.0
When we have conflict, I feel my wife "hears me"	-2.0
I am satisfied with the amount of adventure my wife shows in the bedroom	-1.8
I make my wife's sexual pleasure a priority when we have sex	-1.7
I am comfortable bringing up difficult conversations with my wife	-1.7
My wife makes my sexual pleasure a priority when we have sex	-1.6
I am comfortable talking to my wife about what feels good sexually and what I want sexually	-1.5
I am satisfied with the amount of closeness I share with my wife during sex	-1.4
My wife frequently orgasms during sex	-1.3

Problem #2: Dealing with our Baggage

It may not be the messaging around sex that you struggle with, but the sexual experiences you've had in the past that color your present. Perhaps you're burdened by feelings of guilt because you had sex or fooled around before you were married. Or perhaps you're burdened by quasi-guilt because of what was done to you. Many sexual assault and sexual abuse survivors report feeling guilty, and even though they logically know they weren't responsible, the feeling, and the trauma, won't go away.

And then there are those who had sexual experiences before marriage that were physically very satisfying. When you make love now, you find yourself comparing your husband unfavorably to a past partner. You try to get your hubby to do what the other guy did, and it doesn't work. Too often memories or trauma from past sexual experiences stops you from feeling connected now.

Problem #3: Focus on the Physical

In today's culture, experiencing a deep emotional connection while making love can be a challenge because our brains have gone haywire when it comes to sex. And the culprit isn't hard to find. Too often, just as we start to experience sexual feelings, the first sexual "encounter" we have is with a pornographic image. Maybe it's from a movie or from something we've seen on the internet, but whatever the source, we find ourselves thinking of sex through that prism. Here's what one twenty-eight-year-old woman admitted, "I have a high sex drive, and I love sex. But I find that sex tends to interfere with all the other aspects of the relationship. We spend so much time physically intimate that we don't get emotionally or spiritually intimate."

This woman reports that she and her husband make love almost every day. But here's what's interesting: both of them have used pornography in the past, and for both, sex has become about the physical rather than anything else.

When couples focus only on the physical, they often sense

that they're missing something. Thirty-six percent of women we surveyed who orgasm reliably still said they don't feel emotionally connected during sex. But our culture doesn't give couples the tools to deal with this unsettling feeling. You roll around in bed, and it feels great, but then what? If sex is only for your own pleasure, you may feel as if it is somehow empty.

Problem #4: Fantasizing about Pornographic Images

A few years ago I wrote a series of blog posts to help women whose husbands were addicted to pornography. Then the emails started to arrive. "What about *me*?" all too many women asked. "How do *I* stop looking at the stuff?" Pornography is no longer only a male battle. In one of the surveys I conducted for research for this book, 13 percent of women reported having had trouble with pornography. And when we use it, just like men, our brains become rewired so that we start becoming aroused by a picture rather than by a person.

The Common Barrier to Intimacy: Dissociating during Sex

When sex is seen as something bad, shameful, or threatening, a common defense mechanism is dissociating during sex. For many women, sex doesn't bring them closer to their partners because they're not "present" while making love. Either they leave their bodies and think of something else because they don't like sex, or they fantasize because they can't get aroused otherwise.

Dissociating by "Running Away" from Sex

Clinical psychologist Jennifer Degler explains to a sexual abuse survivor how dissociation works:

> Dissociation temporarily disconnects your mind from your body so that you won't be fully aware of what is being done to your body.

You, like many abuse survivors, are finding that the dissociation continues even though the abuse has stopped, and it is robbing you of a great sex life. In order to enjoy sex with your husband, you have to be connected to your body—feeling, enjoying, and encouraging both his touch and your own body's sexual response. Sexual abuse trains us to not feel, enjoy, or encourage healthy sexual touch or our body's natural responsiveness to sexual stimulation.[1]

If you were sexually abused in the past, you may have tried to think of anything else during the abuse—and taught your mind how to separate from your body. That was your mind protecting you from what was happening to you. Today when you have sex, you still can't seem to "reconnect" your body and your mind.

But it's not only sexual assault survivors who struggle with dissociation. When sex feels emotionally threatening, even if it's because of past messaging or beliefs about sex, integrating your body and mind during sex can be difficult because your mind wants to run away.

Dissociating by Fantasizing

Dissociating isn't only done by checking out of your body during sex; it can also be done by turning to pornographic images or to memories of other partners to get aroused. Perhaps your husband has never figured out how to make you feel good, or perhaps you have other issues, like past sexual baggage, abuse, or physical difficulties. You worry about not being able to respond or to enjoy sex, so you do whatever you can to get yourself in the mood. And frequently that involves pulling up pornographic images or fantasies seared into your brain.

I've received a myriad of emails and brave comments from women saying, "I know I'm dissociating during sex and thinking about anything except what is going on, but I don't know how to stop."

Unfortunately, when you use fantasy to get you through making love, because you're not present in an emotional or spiritual way, you're essentially conceding that sex is only physical. I'm not saying that all fantasy is wrong; thinking occasionally about some great time you and your husband had last year is all good! But fantasizing about strangers or fantasizing about anything that would be considered lust ultimately harms intimacy.

From the emails I've received and responses to my surveys, I know many of you deal with dissociating problems and experience much anguish because of it. Let me use a composite of some of these emails to tell the story of a woman we'll call Christy.

When Christy was eight years old, she was exposed to far more than she should have been one Saturday morning when she accompanied her dad to a barber shop. While the barber trimmed her dad's beard, she thumbed through the stack of magazines on a table, including several issues of *Playboy*. Seeing those pictures made her feel funny.

A few years later, at a sleepover, a friend showed her some strange videos she had on her phone. Those funny feelings returned.

As a teen, she was date-raped. She never told anybody. After all, she told herself, nothing really "bad" happened from it—she wasn't pregnant, and she didn't get an STI—so she decided to put it behind her. She was a Christian, and she wanted to forgive the boy, so she did. Forgive and forget, as they say.

In her midtwenties she married a wonderful Christian man. Before the wedding, they shared breathless make-out sessions, but they didn't go any further. Then, on her wedding night, she froze. Instead of being excited like she was when they were engaged, she felt nothing.

Over time they continued to have intercourse, with Christy desperately hoping her sex drive would return. But she didn't enjoy sex, and she found herself trying to think of anything *but* sex in order to get through it. After a few years, she felt broken. Everybody else was enjoying sex, but she saw it as a chore. Surely she was capable of enjoying sex, wasn't she?

That's when the pictures started to come back. She remembered all those images and videos she had seen and how they had made her feel aroused. One night, curious, she typed some sketchy words into a search engine. Soon she had a bunch more pictures in her head to go along with the ones from her childhood.

The next time she had sex, she thought of those pictures. She found herself getting aroused. She finally felt like she wasn't a freak, like she was normal! And her husband was happy because she enjoyed it.

But she was still separate from her body. She was still "running away" in her mind. Yes, her body was responding, but it was responding because of something she was imagining, not something her husband was doing. Over the years she got better at it. And he didn't know that anything was amiss.

Does that story sound familiar to you? Many women are hurting like this, falling into several categories:

- Those for whom sex is painful or shameful
- Those for whom sex isn't fun, either because the husband doesn't know how to properly stimulate the wife or because they have never bothered to figure out how to make sex work together
- Those who experienced trauma from abuse or assault
- Those who were heavily involved with porn as children, often because someone else showed it to them

These women don't want to disappoint their husbands, and they don't want to feel as if there is something wrong with them because everyone else in the world seems to like sex. So they desperately look for some shortcut to arousal and find it in pornography and fantasy.

If you have engaged in any form of porn use, including an erotica or fantasy addiction, confessing to your husband is part of healing—and it's also the right thing to do. You may need to give him space to heal from any betrayal he may feel. Counselors specifically trained in this can help your husband process this new information.

Overcoming These Problems

While we may have various reasons for our difficulties connecting on a deep, personal level during sex, the solution to all these problems is the same: bring it into the open, work toward healing, and then learn how to retrain your mind and body to feel, think, and respond differently to sex. Often the best route God gives us for healing is through seeing a licensed therapist trained in trauma therapy, and I highly recommend that for anybody with trauma in their pasts. Trauma isn't something you can "get over" by forgiving or having more faith. It causes changes in the brain, giving you triggers that send you back into fight, flight, or freeze mode. Your body tried to be your friend by protecting you when you were experiencing trauma. But now that protection is getting in the way of enjoying sex when you're with your husband. Thankfully, counselors have found evidence-based therapies that can help your brain let go of the panic response and reintegrate into wholeness and can help you disclose this information to your spouse as well if you need the support.

Aside from therapy with a licensed counselor, these steps can also help to retrain you to respond anew to sex.

Healing Step #1: Redeem the Meaning of Sex

If sex has negative connotations for you, chances are you have been hurt in the past, believed bad messages, or have engaged in behavior you regret.* First, ask God to heal your heart from those scars. Ask God to give you a new heart and a new mind when it comes to sexual intimacy.

---

* If negative connotations are because of how your husband is treating you, that's something different. Please seek out a licensed counselor or a domestic abuse hotline, if appropriate.

Other times we have difficulty embracing sex because of the shameful messages around it. Many of us grew up being taught to "stay pure until you're married." But do you notice how that implies that once you're married, you're no longer pure? Having sex seems to rob you of your "purity" because we've defined purity as being about virginity (something that is extra harmful for sexual abuse survivors). If sex was seen as something bad when you were growing up but was supposed to magically become good once you were married, that transition can be tricky. It can also be challenging to see sex as something positive if you've heard the obligation sex message your whole married life. Obligation is the opposite of intimacy. Intimacy says, "I want to know you through sex," which means that both of you matter. Obligation says, "I have to do this for you no matter what I'm feeling," which means that only one person's needs matter. Instead of sex being something that unites you, it feels like something that erases you.

Rejecting these harmful messages is key to embracing your own sexuality. Sex is not a one-sided, ugly obligation. It does not have to be defined by something ugly that was done to you. It does not need to be seen as ugly at all! You're married. Sex is a beautiful thing that is completely and utterly for you too. Whatever your past, God wants to bless you today in the bedroom, even if your parents or your church community never told you this was possible.

> Rejecting these harmful messages is key to embracing your own sexuality.

Healing Step #2: Learn That Your Body Can Respond Sexually

Now it's time to retrain your body! Jennifer Degler gives this promise—with a warning—to her clients: "You *can* retrain yourself to stay connected to your body during sex, but be patient with yourself because it takes a lot of practice!"[2]

Practice being naked together. Since healing can't be rushed, taking baby steps is the best route to enjoying your body anew. Lie naked together. Take baths together. Without any expectation that you will make love that night, enjoy your husband's body. Run your hands over it. Concentrate on the intimacy that comes from doing something you will do only with him. Don't think of this as foreplay; do this separately from intercourse to become more accustomed to being mentally present when you make love. If you get him pretty worked up, you can also help him climax using your hands, if you want to, so that you don't feel pressure to finish with intercourse. Make the point of the evening be to help you feel how intimate it is to be naked together—and to appreciate how he responds to your body!

Play games to learn what feels good. Many women who aren't mentally present during sex, or who don't enjoy sex, like Christy, assume that their sex drives are dead, even those who desire sex a lot because porn has jump-started their libidos. They don't long for their husbands to touch them; they only get turned on by fantasy. If that describes you, let me reassure you that your sex drive is not dead! It has just been transferred elsewhere.

Have confidence that you *can* and *will* experience pleasure one day. After all, your body was created to experience pleasure. Nevertheless, we don't all enjoy the same things, so explore and figure out what you do like. Some women love having their breasts touched; others don't. Some find their ears or their toes are erogenous zones; other women like to focus only on the genitals.

Here are some games to learn about your body.

The Dice Game—Take two different-colored six-sided dice and assign the numbers on one with six body parts (neck, ears, breasts, mouth, genitals, thighs) and one with six actions (lick, kiss, tease gently, stroke firmly, suck, nibble). Then take turns rolling the dice and doing whatever combination comes up, say for one minute each. Sometimes having a prompt to do something new helps you try something you may be too nervous to ask for.

The Timer Game—Set the timer for ten minutes, then let him touch you. Let him use a variety of objects, like a feather, an ice cube, his finger, his tongue. See what you like. This game also helps the men who may never have learned to appreciate the benefits of foreplay to see how aroused they can get their wives. Then do the same thing to your husband. Seeing the reaction you get and feeling the sexual power you have can be erotic.

This process may take several weeks or months as you grow accustomed to relaxing, being present, and learning that your body can indeed respond. You can't rewire your brain overnight. But the wonderful thing about being married is that you have a lot of time ahead of you to practice.

Healing Step #3: Learn to Be Emotionally and Mentally Present

It is a beautiful thing to be present with your husband—body, mind, and soul—when you make love. But if you have difficulty being present, here are some ideas to keep your mind focused.

PAY ATTENTION TO WHAT IS GOING ON

Do you find your mind wandering while you're making love? Stop that train of thought and replace it with this one instead: Ask yourself constantly, "What would I like him to do now?" It sounds silly, as if you're judging his performance, but that's not the point. If you ask yourself, "What would I like him to do?" you'll pay attention to cues your body sends you, and you'll realize that different body parts do want some attention. Dissociation is the act of mentally leaving your body to think about something else. This technique pulls your brain back to the matter at hand.

To reintegrate with your body, deliberately pay attention to what your body is feeling, not just what you are thinking. When your breasts feel like they want some attention or your clitoris gets that tugging feeling, tell him. He'll likely find your desire exciting because he will never have seen you like this before. If you've used most of your intimate experiences in the past to think about other things, or to check out entirely, it means that you weren't as active physically because you weren't paying attention to your body. Once you concentrate on what your body is feeling, you are more engaged in the process.

If something doesn't feel good, tell him that too. Don't just endure it, because for women, paying attention is the key to sexual arousal. And if he's doing something you don't like, it's hard to keep your head in the game. Either tell him what's uncomfortable, or redirect his hand or whatever else he's using to stimulate you.

TALK TO HIM

If you want to stay present, talk. Tell him you love him. Tell him what you like. If you talk, your mind is brought back to the present, and you're more likely to stay in the moment.

LOOK INTO HIS EYES

You can't picture a different image if you're looking into his eyes. And the connection when you do that is intense. Talk to him, look into his eyes, concentrate on what he is doing, and banish any distractions. You'll find that sex is more intimate than it was before, even if you don't achieve orgasm right away. A big sexual high comes simply from feeling connected to your husband, and if you usually dissociate during sex, you may have never experienced the love that truly connects you.

When He's the One Struggling with Images

While many women struggle with porn and erotica, we know that it is an even more common issue among men. And a man's porn use often affects how he sees sex and how he sees and treats his wife, often causing its own trauma and making sex seem ugly. Every morning when I check my emails and comments that came in over overnight, I invariably find at least one email like this one that greeted me today:

> Last night I found porn on my husband's phone. I knew he used porn when he was a teen, but he told me he quit when we started dating. We've been married for seven years now, and I always felt something was off in the bedroom, and now things make sense. He doesn't know I know, and I don't know what to do.

She's not alone in her desperation. When married people use porn, divorce rates double.[3] Sociologists know porn sends marriages crashing, but it can also send guys' libidos through the floor. Slowly but surely a man who uses porn can become less interested in sex with his wife. When he is interested, he may want to try more extreme things, and he can have difficulty having sex without fantasizing.

Even secular researchers are noticing this. Sex and relationship counselor Ian Kerner has coined the term SADD—sexual attention deficit disorder—to describe men who find that porn wrecks their sex lives. Kerner explains, "Just as people with ADD are easily distracted, guys with SADD have become so accustomed to the high levels of visual novelty and stimulation that comes from internet porn that they're unable to focus on real sex with a real woman."[4]

Porn is the most common problem I get asked about, and it is devastating marriages—especially younger ones. Our men's survey found that 73.4 percent of husbands report that porn has been an issue for them *at some point,* though thankfully most do put porn use behind them. Today, 6.5 percent of men in our survey reported using porn on a regular basis (daily or weekly), 16.7 percent have intermittent binges, and another 26.5 percent use it rarely. And although it is not the case for all, for far too many, porn affects their view of sex, damages their view of women, and interferes with intimacy and even sexual function. And, to put it even more bluntly, porn use brings infidelity into the marriage.

I like to think of responding to porn use the way you would a cancerous mole. It always needs to get checked out as soon as possible. It always needs to be fully removed. But not all cancerous moles turn into metastatic melanomas. Some, however, do. And to ignore a mole because, well, *it's only one* or *it'll probably be fine* is unwise.

Too often we minimize porn use, thinking that if he's sorry and he promises never to do it again, everything will be okay. We're told in the church to forgive quickly, and so we try to move on. But porn use can have devastating consequences and can cause men to develop a "pornographic style of relating," as counselor Andrew J. Bauman calls it.[5] Instead of honoring women as the *imago Dei*, as whole people made in the image of God, men with a pornographic style of relating often view their wives, and even other women, as objects to be consumed, or objects they are entitled to use for their own gratification. You cannot build intimacy or a healthy marriage until this is properly dealt with.

You Did Not Cause His Porn Use—and You Can't Fix It

The good news is that not only is his porn use not your fault; it's also not your responsibility. You cannot fix his porn use by having more sex—because that just reinforces the pornographic style of relating by reducing sex to simply a numbing agent for his temptation. You cannot fix it by being sexier—because, again, the problem is that he has trained his sexual response to react to objectification rather than

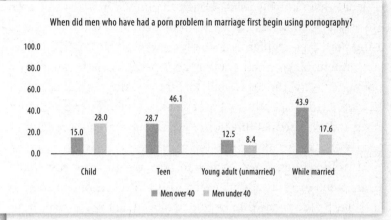

When did men who have had a porn problem in marriage first begin using pornography?

Child: Men over 40 = 15.0, Men under 40 = 28.0
Teen: Men over 40 = 28.7, Men under 40 = 46.1
Young adult (unmarried): Men over 40 = 12.5, Men under 40 = 8.4
While married: Men over 40 = 43.9, Men under 40 = 17.6

■ Men over 40 ■ Men under 40

to intimacy. *You cannot fix this because you did not cause it.* Too often women have been blamed for husbands' porn use, as if he's turning to porn because you're rejecting him. But most men under the age of forty actually started their porn habits before they even met their wives! If your husband uses porn, it has nothing to do with you.

Any porn use must be dealt with before you work on your sex life so that he can rediscover intimacy and reawaken healthy desire. Instead of opening himself up to the intimacy and vulnerability required for real relationships, the porn user feels the high that porn brings while preserving a false image of himself.[6] Porn allows him to hide his emotions by experiencing a high through porn instead of through intimacy. If your marriage is going to recover, he has to stop hiding.

That's why you can't break that addiction by becoming sexier and more outlandish; if you do that, you'll cement the addiction. You are not responsible for him using porn, and having sex constantly will not break that habit. Sex and porn are not substitutes for each other. Sex is a deep "knowing," an intimate joining. Porn is dehumanizing, a "using," and it cannot be tolerated—not least because it is so highly linked to sex trafficking and often depicts sexual assaults.

You Can Say No to Porn in Your Marriage

Sarah McDugal, an abuse recovery coach who works with women healing after betrayal trauma, tells her clients, "You cannot control what your husband does or the choices he makes. However, you have the right to live in a home free of pornography and explicit material. You have the right to live in a marriage free of betrayal. You have the right to exist in safety on a daily basis. When your husband is using porn he is violating your rights to safety, trust, and intimacy."[7] And it is okay to take a firm stand against porn.

Your husband needs to take full responsibility for and initiative in pursuing his porn recovery. That's not something you can do for him. He needs to decide it's wrong, he needs to go to God in repentance, and he needs to pursue help, most likely from a counselor or recovery group, to deal with any emotional stuntedness the porn habit has caused. He can't "white knuckle" through a porn addiction and simply try harder. He needs to address his wounds and learn intimacy. Andrew Bauman, cofounder of the Christian Counseling Center for Sexual Health and Trauma, believes that healing is best done in community. "Community doesn't just mean accountability, it means bleeding together; it means sharing our deepest shame, greatest fears, and deepest delights. True communion is fully knowing and being fully known by another."[8] It's that "knowing" and that openness that allow for transformation.

> You can't break that addiction by becoming sexier and more outlandish.

You can't do the work for him, and if he refuses to do the work, then you'll have to decide what you want to do with the relationship. But even if he does do the work, you may need some help too. Many spouses of porn users suffer from betrayal trauma, with symptoms similar to post traumatic stress disorder. Working through this with a licensed counselor will help you make an informed decision about how you want to proceed with the relationship. However, there are porn-addicted husbands who have allowed pornography to so warp their sexuality and their view of women that their wives cannot feel safe with them again, even if they promise to get help. In these cases, the betrayal is so serious that the marriage cannot be saved, and this should not be seen as a failure on the part of the betrayed spouse.

Rebuilding Your Marriage and Your Sex Life

I know that all sounds bleak, but when we don't treat porn seriously enough it can fester, and intimacy can remain elusive (while betrayal can keep recurring). I don't want to leave you feeling like this is helpless, though, because in most cases it's not. Though many men have had a porn problem, marriages where the porn user is fully repentant and takes complete ownership of his behavior as well as his treatment are often able to put it behind them and recover.

When Kayla's husband, Doug, confessed his porn use on their seventeenth anniversary, Kayla was devastated. Over the next few years, they sought counseling individually, he joined recovery groups, he confessed to his family members, and he slowly rebuilt trust. But Kayla found that the last bit of healing actually came on her son's birthday. As she put eleven candles on the cake and placed it in front of her smiling preteen, she experienced a big jolt. He was still so small. He still played with Legos. And he was exactly the same age her husband had been when he found *Playboy* magazines in the ditch on his way to school. She realized that porn didn't just steal the first part of their marriage—it also stole her husband's childhood and teenage years. It stole his innocence. And by fervently pursuing recovery, Doug was also learning to forgive the scared, ashamed, and confused little boy who found a magazine on the side of the road.

Actor Terry Crews made headlines when he went public with his porn addiction in 2016. He and his wife, Rebecca, a Christian speaker, have told their story of a marriage nearly breaking apart and the recovery they experienced instead.

When Terry admitted to Rebecca that he had a porn addiction, accompanied by using a prostitute, she told him the marriage was over.* Vows had been broken; she couldn't see a way back from that. That was the wake-up call Terry needed. He made the commitment to get better, even if he still lost the marriage.[9] He sought help from therapists who helped him find the root of his addiction. His sex addiction had nothing to do with his wife; it was the way he had become accustomed to dealing with his pain. It was his way of running away from intimacy, and now he couldn't hide anymore. Seeing Terry's earnestness to recover, Rebecca didn't jump right back into the marriage, but she did decide to give him a chance to rebuild, with strict rules, including absolutely no porn use or infidelity of any sort.

After attending therapy, Terry asked his wife to try a sex fast—ninety days with no sex but a lot of communication. In a video, Rebecca Crews explained that they did the sex fast to try to reestablish intimacy apart from sex. Because of Terry's porn addiction, sex had become depersonalized. They'd have sex, but it wasn't emotionally or spiritually intimate, and it left her feeling hollow and empty. But when they did the fast? Rebecca says: "The sex fast made us like teenagers again. We began to talk to each other; we kissed without expecting it to turn into something."[10]

The first time they tried the sex fast they only made it to seventy-five days, but Terry came back the next year and wanted to make

---

* Terry's story is a serious case of sex addiction that escalated to real-life acting out. His story is not meant as an example of which marriages can or should be rebuilt, but only as an example of what real repentance looks like. I'm sharing Terry's story, although it is extreme, because he's a public figure who has done so much to raise awareness of the harms of sex addiction and what is healthy sexuality.

it to ninety. "I was so serious about our marriage, about improving who I was."[11] He wanted to discover true intimacy, and that's what they did—because he decided he was done with porn, because he took his sex addiction seriously, and because they got qualified help. Terry was able to stop hiding and learn that vulnerability and sexuality could be, and should be, intrinsically linked.

That's the aim: being able to be completely comfortable with each other, focusing on each other, and being present with each other. It's an absolute tragedy that so much in our culture, and especially pornography, works directly against that. God wants true intimacy for us, and if something in your life is stealing it or distorting it, please get whatever help you need to find it.

CHAPTER 6

A Pure, Holy, and Hot Marriage

If there are two words not exactly linked in the Christian mindset, they would be *holy* and *hot*. I don't think that's because God separated them; I think it's because we did. We don't understand how God designed sex to be passionate and how that passion, when properly channeled, is a good thing.

In the last chapter, we looked at some barriers to "holy" sex: we have a hard time seeing sex in a positive light or enjoying our spouses because we struggle with pornographic images or other flashbacks, or he makes sex ugly in our relationship because of his own pornography use. But what does "holy" sex mean? With so much working against a healthy and holy view of sex, how can we begin to understand this? And is it even possible to be holy and hot at the same time? Actually, I think that's the biblical view of sex. It's purity and passion together, and that's what makes it so wonderful.

I know many of us have had major obstacles to overcome to see sex in a holistic and holy way. I hope in this chapter to give you a more complete vision of what God meant for sex—no more ugliness, no more using, no more shame. Just true intimacy, passion, and connection.

Let's start with what *holiness* means in a Christian marriage context, and then we'll see how that leads to truly intimate, mind-blowing passion.

Holy Sex: Learning to Make Love

Most of us have had sex to say, "I want you." We've had sex because we want to relax, have fun, or experience fireworks. But too few couples have had sex to say, "I love you." What is truly sexy, and what brings true bliss in the bedroom, is not *just* becoming multi-orgasmic. It's not being able to do sexual gymnastics or being able to last for three hours at a time. It's something much more profound. It's a feeling of not knowing where your spouse ends and where you begin.

> Making love is a feeling of not knowing where your spouse ends and where you begin.

For those of you who are married, have you ever felt like you are saying, "I love you," when you have sex? Or has it been mostly about physical pleasure? Feeling love involves paying attention and thinking about your spouse while you are connected. One survey respondent opened a rather beautiful, intimate window into her life that illustrates this intention perfectly:

> Early in our marriage we were at a marriage conference where the speaker said that orgasm was a lot like imprinting. You know how little baby geese follow around whomever they see as soon as they are born? What they see first when they're born gets imprinted. And it's the same with us and orgasm. What we hear gets imprinted.
>
> So my husband decided (without telling me) that every time

he orgasmed, and every time I orgasmed, he was going to say, "I love you, Becky." He wanted those words to become the erotic ones in our marriage. So no matter how hot the sex is, even if we're being rather raunchy, he always says, "I love you, Becky," at that exact moment. He uses my name. And now sometimes he just leans over to me during the day and whispers it in my ear, and it definitely gives me warm fuzzies!

Saying "I love you" when you make love is such a simple thing. But it helps you focus on *why* you're making love. Look each other in the eyes. Say each other's names. Kiss each other and that emotional and spiritual connection becomes much deeper. That's the connection you're looking for—not only physical pleasure but also feeling as if you complete each other.

Katelyn has spent many hours in trauma counseling dealing with childhood sexual abuse and has experienced tremendous healing in her life. But she feels like God has used her husband—even their sex life—as a balm to her wounds. She told me, "Occasionally I still have flashbacks from my childhood trauma. When I do, I've learned to share the memory with Bryan. He validates that it was abuse and should have never happened, and then I'm able to process the emotions of that while he holds me close. Those times have led to the most healing kind of love-making. It's helped me overcome a lot of my childhood trauma." As Katelyn was vulnerable, and let her husband enter into her deepest emotions, they began to express physically what their hearts already felt.

When we're vulnerable with our mates, we feel a deep sense of connection because we vow that we are in this together. And that connection can be powerful. Sexually, it becomes an urgency to devour your husband, to consume him, to be consumed by him just so that you can feel even more connected. God put that hunger in us to yearn for each other. In many ways, that hunger reflects how God feels about you.

Understanding God's Passion

It may seem strange to bring God into a discussion on passionate sex, but God designed sex to mirror his relationship with us. We are the bride being prepared for the bridegroom.

Renaissance poets expressed this quite well. Listen to what Shakespeare's contemporary, John Donne, wrote to God in his sonnet "Batter My Heart":

> Batter my heart, three-person'd God, for you
> As yet but knock, breathe, shine, and seek to mend;
> That I may rise and stand, o'erthrow me, and bend
> Your force, to break, blow, burn, and make me new.
>
> . . . .
>
> Take me to you, imprison me, for I,
> Except you enthrall me, never shall be free,
> Nor ever chaste, except you ravish me.[1]

Donne is asking God to overthrow him, to bend him, to break him, to conquer him. He's saying, "I'll never be chaste unless you ravish me." Does that sound like a nice orderly relationship in which no one ever loses control? Not to me. It's a tale of bending completely to another who overpowers you. That sounds a lot like passionate sex!

But John Donne wasn't some pervert. He was expressing the same thing the apostle Paul expressed when he wrote in Galatians 2:20: "I have been crucified with Christ and I no longer live, but Christ lives in me. The life I now live in the body, I live by faith in the Son of God, who loved me and gave himself for me."

We are not alone; we carry God in our bodies, and we want more of him and less of us. "He must become greater; I must become less," John the Baptist said of Jesus (John 3:30). We yearn for God, and not only for his presence but for a deeply intimate relationship in which he *does* overpower us, in which he *does* consume us, in which we no longer feel alone, but so imbued with him that we are finally complete.

That is how we feel about God and how he feels about us. He uses sex as imagery for the deep hunger we have for a spiritual union with God. We hunger to be completed by God, and God made us so that we hunger in a similar way for each other. Maybe it's no wonder that in the height of sexual tension, many women long to be "devoured," to be "taken"!

Bringing God In

Unfortunately, some in the Christian church have promulgated a bizarre and dangerous belief that God and sex don't go together. They think sex God's way must banish all the carnal desire, messiness, and awkwardness.

But God designed sex with that messiness, awkwardness, and carnal desire. And I think he did it because our union is supposed to be messy and emotional and a little bit out of control. As C. S. Lewis said of the Narnian Christ figure, Aslan—he's not a tame lion.[2] And our union with God isn't tame either. The closer we get to God, the more intense our passions.

That's why sex isn't sterile. It isn't supposed to be, any more than our relationship with God is supposed to be all neat and tidy and easily understandable. And so sex isn't shameful before God. Rather, I think God probably laughs when we lose control when we're making love— when we surrender, when we lose our ability to think clearly, even when we scream right before climax—because that's what we also feel when we draw close to him. Vulnerability is part of an intimate relationship.

Sex with God on our side means a lot of surrender and a lot of fun! And sex is even greater when you bring God into it. He cares about you being able to fully give yourself to your husband. He cares about how great it feels because he made it that way. And there's no time I want to make love with my husband more than after we've prayed together, especially for our kids. When I see my husband surrender himself to God and ask for God to work in our kids' lives, I want him in every way.

> Sex is even greater when you bring God into it.

The spiritual bliss we're supposed to feel from sex comes from a union built on physical desire fueled by a friendship that brings trust and laughter but culminates in a beautiful longing for the other. Let's take that longing and act on it.

Pure Passion: The Intersection between Holy and Hunger

While the intersection between the holy and sexual hunger sounds intriguing and exciting, the practical living out of this passion can be a land mine for Christians. We want to build a spiritual union in which we deeply desire each other, lose control, and experience tremendous fireworks, but does it matter how those fireworks are exploded?

Yep, it does. The most common questions I'm asked through my blog and podcast are about specific sexual activities. Is oral sex okay? What about lingerie? What about sex toys? I know these are important questions, but sometimes they leave me rather sad because we sometimes focus on the wrong thing: we look at specific physical acts instead of the relationship as a whole.

Personally, I believe in freedom in marriage. God made sex to feel amazing as a gift, and he rejoices when we enjoy it. But I want to offer a word of caution. Many "extra" sexual practices have become mainstream over the last few decades because pornography is so rampant. These stem from the unhealthy sexual attitude that sex is about pushing physical boundaries. One of the problems with getting *too* focused on these extra sexual practices is that couples miss out on the beauty of just being together, especially early in marriage.

We even risk making sex into an idol. The verse that is often quoted at marriage conferences about giving to each other, 1 Corinthians 7:5, says, "Do not deprive each other except perhaps by mutual consent and for a time, so that you may devote yourselves to prayer. Then come together again so that Satan will not tempt you because of your lack of self-control."

We like to focus on the "do not deprive each other" part of the verse to stress that we should be having regular sexual relations and satisfying our spouses. It goes right along with verse 4: "The wife does not have authority over her own body but yields it to her husband. In the same way, the husband does not have authority over his own body but yields it to his wife." We belong to each other, so let's have sex!

Yes, these verses affirm that sex is good and that we should make love regularly. After all, fasting from sex wouldn't work to drive us to God if we didn't also enjoy and yearn for sex. Yet we're often unwilling to look at the other ramification of that verse: *the fasting itself is part of a healthy Christian marriage.* In modern Christian writing and speaking on sex, we're far more comfortable debating what practices are and aren't okay and how to have the best sex possible than we are talking about how our devotion to God fits into our sexual relationship.

> Fasting itself is part of a healthy Christian marriage.

Sex has become all about how to have the most amount of fun. While God made it to be fun, he also made us to yearn for him, and even though sex mimics that yearning, sex doesn't replace it. If you already have regular and passionate sex, your intimate lives would be more enhanced by spending time praying fervently together in bed and then coming together at the end rather explosively than they would by pushing the boundaries of what's okay and what's not.

So, please, as you read this chapter, take this as its context: God wants us to enjoy our bodies. He wants us to feel completely one, to yearn for each other, to reach those explosive heights. But this should never replace our yearning for him, and in that yearning, we will likely yearn for each other more too. The key to a passionate marriage is not to be as sexually adventurous as possible but to be as passionate about God and about life as possible. As we come close to him, we'll experience more freedom and more energy in the bedroom.

How Do You Decide What's Okay?

Now let's turn to the parameters we've learned about to decide what activities are okay. God designed sex to re-create in a physical way the longing that we have to be joined to him. That longing is wrapped up in the feelings of being incredibly loved and cherished, of amazing pleasure, of becoming supremely vulnerable. And in all of that, there is no coercion. There is no unhealthy fear. Thus, for a sexual relationship to express that spiritual connection, it can't be something scary or domineering because God does not express his relationship to us that way. That means that consent matters—even in marriage!

> Consent matters— even in marriage!

What Does Consent Look Like?

Nonconsensual sex occurs any time a person feels they cannot say no. If you can't say no, then you can't truly say yes. One of the most heartbreaking parts of my job is opening emails and reading stories of sexual assault in marriage. And what's even worse is that many women don't realize that it *is* assault, or that rape in marriage can happen. Too many women think we aren't allowed to say no because the Bible tells us "do not deprive." If he wants sex, you have no choice. One reader told me, "I lost track of how many times I went to church leadership for help, and they all said the same thing: 'Marital rape is not possible. You need to get your heart right.'" But marital rape is possible, and if this is your story, the problem is not with you. It's with your husband.

Some coercion is easier to spot because you're physically held down and constrained. But coercion can be more subtle—and still be coercion. Any time you don't feel free to say no because something bad will likely happen, sex is not consensual.

- If your husband withholds money, gives you the silent treatment, or is irritable or angry with you if you don't have sex or perform certain sexual acts, that's coercion.
- If he uses a sex toy on you without your consent, has sex with you while you're sleeping, or does something that you've already said you don't want, that's assault, even if you become aroused or have an orgasm from that act.[3]
- If after he has sex with you, he yells at you less, or yells at the children less, so you feel as if you have to have sex to manage his moods and keep others safe, that's coercion.
- If he uses Bible verses as a weapon against you, that's coercion, and it's also spiritually abusive.
- If he tells you that the only way he can stop watching porn or lusting or having an affair is if you have sex with him, then that's coercion.

One woman wrote to me saying that she had to be sure to have sex with her husband every week before their small group met at their house because otherwise he'd be grumpy, make inappropriate comments, and embarrass her in front of their friends. She also had to have sex with him before they took the kids on a big family outing, like to the beach, or else he'd yell at the kids in frustration and refuse to help. If you recognize yourself in these stories, please see a licensed counselor, or call a domestic violence hotline if you feel like you're in immediate danger.[4]

Guidelines for Deciding Your Boundaries in the Bedroom

I hope coercion isn't a part of your marriage, but consent is crucial for all of us to understand.

Now, assuming coercion isn't a factor and we're simply wondering about how to have more fun, how do we decide our boundaries? We know sex must be voluntary, but we also know it's not tame. Let's look at some guidelines that logically follow:

1. You're married. You're allowed to do stuff! Freedom and liberty are themes of the Christian life (Galatians 5:1).
2. Sex should not be something that makes one person feel degraded or uncomfortable (Philippians 2:3–4).
3. If you or your husband don't want to do something, don't do it. Both parties must always be 100 percent willing, or you shouldn't do it (1 Corinthians 7:3–5).
4. Sex should always involve only the two of you. If you're fantasizing about someone else, or if he's fantasizing about someone else, it's wrong, even if you're physically acting it out with your husband (see Matthew 5:28).

And finally, the one that sums up the whole thing:

5. Sex should be something that enhances intimacy, not detracts from it. What you do in the bedroom should make

you feel closer, more known, more loved—not less known, less loved, or used.

How do we apply these guidelines to specific acts? Let's look at some of the most common questions.

WHAT ABOUT ORAL SEX?

Let's be honest here, girls: most men, and most women, enjoy oral sex. While this may once have been considered an outlandish sexual activity, it's now pretty much mainstream. For instance, the National Survey of Sexual Health reported in the October 2010 *Journal of Sexual Medicine* that 76 percent of women ages twenty-five to twenty-nine gave sex orally to a man in the last year, and 72 percent received (versus 87 percent who had experienced vaginal intercourse). Now, just because most people do it is no reason to think that you should. I share those percentages with you not to tell you that you *should* have oral sex but to show that your husband is not a weird pervert if he's interested in it (and neither are you if it is something you enjoy).

Nevertheless, some Christians object because it's focused on one person's pleasure rather than experiencing pleasure together, but I don't find that a persuasive argument. Giving is a good thing, not a bad thing. And some believe that his ejaculating anywhere other than inside her vagina (so that the potential for procreation is preserved) is also wrong. But even then, you can always start one way and finish another!

Ultimately, I think oral sex comes down to personal preference. Because sex is supposed to be something that connects you together, if you feel degraded or ashamed, or even uncomfortable, it's not worth it. But if you want to try it, there aren't biblical injunctions against it. You can even make the case that Song of Songs 2:3, "his fruit is sweet to my taste," alludes to oral sex.

What, exactly, does oral sex involve? When oral sex is performed on a guy, it usually involves his wife kissing, licking, and sucking his penis as she moves her mouth up and down its shaft. This doesn't have to be the whole sexual encounter. If you find the thought of kissing his penis attractive, but the thought of him ejaculating while you do it terrifies you, then simply use oral sex as foreplay.

When you're on the receiving end, oral sex usually involves your husband using his tongue to stimulate your clitoris—and even your vagina. It's really no different from him kissing your nipples or other erogenous zones. They're all part of your body, after all. Yet while oral stimulation can be very enjoyable, many women balk at it because they're embarrassed. *What if I'm smelly down there? And what about all the hair?* The smell can be taken care of by washing, and there isn't hair on the clitoris or vagina, only around it. And keeping your hair clipped shorter around the labia minora (the inner lips where your clitoris and vagina are) may relieve some hesitation.

But if it's not your thing and you find the whole thought distasteful, then you don't need to try it. That would detract from intimacy, not enhance it. It's far more important to find things you enjoy and are comfortable doing and to do those with as much gusto as you can muster than to try everything under the sun.

WHAT ABOUT ANAL SEX?

While oral sex is more mainstream, anal sex is not, though its popularity is growing. I don't think the Bible speaks directly to the issue within marriage. Nevertheless, biblical injunction or not, we see anal sex in a very different category than oral sex.

Anal sex, after all, can cause injury. It comes with a higher risk of tearing and spreading disease. While the anus may be an opening in the body, the similarities with the vagina pretty much stop there. It's not like one's a front door and one's a back door; one may be a door, but the other is more like a sewage drain.

And they're anatomically distinct. The vagina has many nerve endings; the rectum has few. The rectum is part of the digestive system and was designed to absorb material, which is why spreading disease is easier. The vagina has a low pH to kill germs; the rectum has a neutral to high pH. The vagina's epithelium is relatively thick and is highly elastic, whereas the rectum's is quite thin and less elastic. If you're going to engage in any kind of anal play, you have to be much more careful with cleanliness, and never switch from anal to vaginal sex without washing well or switching condoms, since spreading bacteria from the anus to the vagina can cause infections.

Does this mean you can't have anal sex? I don't think the Bible explicitly forbids it, but I do believe it's becoming more popular because anything that pushes limits is now considered sexy. So if you feel tempted to try it, or if your husband wants it, ask yourself why. Is it because you want to feel closer together, or is it because you've bought into what the pornographic culture says is sexy? If it's the latter, exercise caution because it may feed into a view of sex that's a hindrance to intimacy rather than a help.

CAN WE USE SEX TOYS?

Popping up all over my region is a chain of stores called Aren't We Naughty? While sex shops used to be lewd, dark places on back streets, these are bright, clean stores in strip malls. Sex toys have become mainstream.

Are they okay? Again, there are no specific biblical injunctions against sex toys like vibrators or rings or things you insert; freedom is part of a grace-filled marriage. But we must take this in the spirit of "everything is permissible for me, but not everything is beneficial" (1 Corinthians 6:12 BSB). Here's my problem with a lot of toys: many of them re-create body parts (specifically his) in unrealistic ways. Take the common vibrator, for instance, which is designed for clitoral stimulation. It vibrates rapidly at just the right frequency to send many women over the edge.

But many women have lamented to me that they can orgasm with a vibrator but not with their husband. Vibrators provide intense, direct stimulation that no guy can compete with. And sometimes, when reaching orgasm is more difficult, the couple relies on a vibrator because it gets her there faster, rather than working on unlocking her sexual responsiveness in other ways.

As one of my blog commenters said,

> Now two years on since experiencing my first orgasm, my husband prefers using the vibrator all the time and not even trying to figure out my body or mind or how to arouse me. He's a very techie/machine-oriented guy and will outsource any work he can in any area of his life if it means he has to physically/mentally/emotionally do less of the heavy lifting. Plus, we have three small children, so time is never on our side. We'd both rather sleep more right now than have a 1+ hour sex session (which is bare minimum what it would take to get me there without a vibrator). Even though I'm grateful he wants me to orgasm, the more time passes, the more I hate only being able to orgasm from a vibrator. It's about his willingness to put in the time and effort into me. It's really depressing. At the time, I'll accept the vibrator orgasm because I'm so desperate, but the next day I always regret it because I want something more where he actually tries to understand my body. I feel unloved and like he doesn't think I'm worth the time it takes to make me orgasm.

Shortcuts, over the long run, can backfire. Instead of enhancing intimacy, they can detract from it. Many women orgasm easily with a vibrator, and so some couples turn to them when orgasm is difficult. But getting to the bottom of *why* she has difficulty reaching orgasm will likely enhance intimacy more in the long run. Does he need to learn about her body? Does she need to learn to relax? Do they need to work on relationship issues that are making her feel distant?

On the other hand, some women swear by vibrators because orgasm takes so long, and they want their pleasure too. They know they can orgasm in other ways, but they'd prefer it not take as long. And then there are women who just want a breakthrough. If you've been married for decades and can't reach orgasm, often the vibrator can be the one thing that helps you get there and discover what it feels like and what you need to aim for.

I am not saying all sex toys are wrong, but I do think we need to ask ourselves whether something is moving us toward greater intimacy or away from it. Practicing his foreplay techniques and learning your own arousal levels may be a better strategy than to turn to a toy that practically guarantees you orgasm with *it*, but not necessarily with *him*.

CAN I WEAR LINGERIE?

I love lingerie. It's pretty. Even the skimpy ones can hide a multitude of sins, like stretch marks or a tummy or cellulite. Most of us feel more confident with something on rather than being completely naked, and the act of taking something off—slowly—is highly erotic to men.

So, I say, jump in with the lingerie! Your husband is highly visual, and the only naked woman he is allowed to look at is you. Make it worth his while by varying what you wear to bed. You can even text him and tell him what to anticipate.

Lingerie gets a bad rap, I think because it is associated with prostitutes or with role-playing. My friend Karen says one question that often comes up in her circle is when does lingerie become a costume? And are costumes bad? I think the answer to that has to do with how we feel about role-playing, so let's turn to that now.

WHAT ABOUT BONDAGE AND S&M?

There's a huge difference between tying someone up and teasing them so that sensation is heightened and tying them up and degrading them. If you have to emotionally distance yourself from your spouse to get turned on, or if degrading or humiliating someone else turns you on, that is a problem. That isn't real passion; that's counterfeit, and it's cruel, objectifying, and wrong. Playing and teasing are great! Humiliating is not. Communicate openly so that you each understand when that line is crossed for either of you.

WHAT ABOUT TAKING SEXY PHOTOS OR VIDEOS OF EACH OTHER?

You know porn is wrong because you're watching other people have sex. But what about taking pictures of yourselves? If your husband wants to shoot some naked pictures of you, or you of him, or even some pictures of both of you together, is that wrong?

No, I personally don't think so. You are married, and it is perfectly okay to love looking at each other's bodies and to become aroused at what you can do together.

But I do see two red flags: one is spiritual, and the other is practical. On the spiritual side, if he's been a porn user and he wants to re-create what he's seen elsewhere, then doing so could feed his improper view of sexuality. Yes, sex should be exciting, but if he needs to objectify you to become aroused, be careful.

Now what about the practical problem? You wouldn't want such pictures falling into anyone else's hands, especially your children's. What if tomorrow you were to die in an accident and your kids found these images? Or your best friend? Or your mom? What if the kids have the password for your phone and browse your photos? There are some pretty obvious privacy issues you need to be aware of and to consider carefully. Even outside the "is this permissible" issue, there's also a wisdom issue and a safety issue for your children (who don't ever, ever want to see that!).

If you do want to take pictures, I'd suggest having fun posing, let him look at you from all angles, look at the pictures afterward, and then delete them right away.

IS IT OKAY TO MASTURBATE?

Masturbation is the dirty little secret in many people's backgrounds, and that's exactly how we see it: as something dirty. When we masturbate, we fantasize, and fantasy is lust. Therefore masturbation is wrong, isn't it?

Well, yes. And no. Let's go back to first principles with marriage again to figure this one out. Masturbation in marriage can be divided into two categories: (1) solo masturbation for sexual release that shortcuts intimacy and (2) masturbation for sexual pleasure with our partners. The first category is how we typically view masturbation: it's done in secret when one is aroused and craves release. The compulsive pornography user, for instance, always masturbates to the images he or she sees. This kind of masturbation is wrong because it's pure and simple lust.

But that's not the only reason masturbating in secret is wrong. It also steals sexual energy from your spouse. One woman, married fifteen years, knows this from experience. She writes,

> I basically refused my husband sexually for ten plus years. But, selfishly, for the last five plus years of that time, I was masturbating to orgasm pretty much daily. I am now at 150 weeks "clean," but we are still struggling in our sexual relationship.
>
> It occurred to me the other day that maybe one of the reasons I struggle so much when I do not orgasm with my husband goes back to all that masturbation. It's kind of like how pornography affects people, how they become unable to have a healthy sexual relationship with a real person.

When we turn to masturbation instead of our husbands, it affects our ability to respond to them. Let's face it: a female orgasm is awfully tricky. You have to apply just the right amount of pressure on the clitoris for just the right amount of time, every now and then varying the rhythm. Most women could bring themselves to orgasm much faster than their husbands could (though it wouldn't be as emotionally satisfying). And if you do this often enough, as this woman did, your body will likely crave stimulation that your husband can't replicate. You crave the shortcut to orgasm rather than the intimate experience you share together. Masturbation in secret can deaden your desire for your husband.

Yet what if your husband consistently refuses you? What about masturbating simply because you have a deep need that isn't being met?

Masturbation will not help the situation. It may offer temporary physical relief, but it will make you feel even more distant from your husband because you're not achieving the intimacy you want with him. If you enjoy masturbation, you might look forward to the times when he's not home so you can be by yourself. Little can be more poisonous to a marriage. Yes, marriage is difficult when you feel sexually rejected, but the solution is to allow that frustration to spur you on to try to fix the chasm between the two of you.

Nevertheless, the problem masturbation poses to a marriage usually relates more to the *secrecy* than to the act itself. The secrecy cuts you off from your spouse and further eats into the spiritual union you should have. When secrecy isn't a factor, masturbation may be part of the fun in your marriage. Many couples separated by business trips for long periods of time, for instance, engage in "phone sex," where they talk to each other while masturbating. They release tension and giggle about it afterward. They're doing something together, they're each fully aware of what the other is doing, they're fantasizing about each other, and they're helping each other get sexual release, even if it isn't in a traditional way.

Some couples also use masturbation as part of their sexual play in bed, with some major benefits. If you can show each other how you like to be touched, pleasuring your spouse is easier. And putting a finger on your clitoris during intercourse to provide stimulation is not masturbating! It's part of sexual play. Finally, when health issues prevent or inhibit vaginal intercourse, mastur-bation can help you maintain intimacy and still experience sexual release, especially if you touch each other as well. So ask yourself: Are we using masturbation to grow intimacy, or to run away from it? When it does not deprive your spouse of anything—such as intercourse or a sexual outlet—then it can be a tool for enhancing your sex life. If you use masturbation so that you don't need your spouse, or when you prefer masturbation to intercourse and thus deny your spouse intercourse (when health issues aren't involved), it becomes a problem. And if your husband prefers masturbation to sex with you? That isn't okay. Please talk to a licensed counselor and get some help.

Final Thoughts

This chapter can't be an exhaustive list of all the sexual acts I'm frequently questioned about—there are too many! But I hope you have a picture of how to evaluate their benefits or hazards: if it is harmful, hurtful, sinful, or coerced, it's wrong. If it enhances play and intimacy, does not degrade, does not promote promiscuity, and is mutually agreed upon, it's not only fine but is actually part of a pure, intimate marriage and something to be celebrated together.

Now let's turn to the next important stage in your sexual jour-ney: nurturing your friendship so you learn to laugh!

Relational
Intimacy

CHAPTER 7

Becoming Best Friends

Early in our marriage, Keith and I watched a movie in which a fun-loving couple added the words *in bed* to the end of any Chinese fortune, giving that fortune an entirely new meaning. We decided the game sounded fun, so since then, whenever we visit a Chinese restaurant, we eagerly crack open the cookies the instant the bill comes. We've saved hundreds over the years. Here are just a few (you'll have to add the words *in bed* yourself):

- You have the ability to be very persuasive.
- Know the right moment and make your move.
- You have both a lot of ideas and the energy to put them into action.
- It is time to help a friend in need.
- You tend to draw out the talent in others.
- Be content with your lot. One cannot be first in everything.
- You have unusual equipment for success. Use it wisely.
- You possess an excellent imagination.
- Use your talents. That's what they are intended for.
- A focused mind is one of the most powerful forces in the universe.
- Fight for it. You will come out on top.
- You work best when meticulous attention to detail is called for.

- The measure of time to your next goal is the measure of your discipline.
- If your feet are firmly planted, you cannot be moved.
- You can't expect to be a lucky dog if you're always growling.

No matter what mood we're in, if we find a "good" fortune, we smile. Having these little jokes that can turn up at odd times throughout the week makes you laugh together and reminds you that you are connected in a unique way to this person—and only to this person. It's a whole different kind of fun.

Building Fun into Your Marriage

We need fun in our relationships. Without laughter, sex becomes far too serious. With laughter, we create shared intimacies and a closer bond. We need that closer bond to prevent sex from becoming, as C. S. Lewis said, a "false goddess."[1] Sex isn't the basis for our relationship; it's the culmination of everything else, especially the friendship we share.

That's one of the reasons, incidentally, why it's so important to save sex for marriage. When delaying gratification during your dating months and years, you naturally spend the time doing activities other than just making out. You take up biking. You play games. You listen to music. You find hobbies together. You serve together. You form common interests, and you talk about all kinds of things and become closely connected.

But then you marry, and often these activities fall by the wayside because now you can *do it*! And if the sex isn't perfect, then you feel as if you've somehow failed.

You haven't. You're simply still on a journey toward increased intimacy, and the more that you can give yourself a break in the physical realm and keep working on your friendship, the more the physical side will be fun too. And the easier time you'll have feeling a spiritual connection. You'll be able to relax and to give and receive more easily. And relaxation is the key to a woman's sexual response.

Couples who focus too much on orgasm and not enough on friendship don't tend to have satisfying sex lives because they've forgotten that it's not just about body parts; it's about the relationship. And when couples are trying to recover from pornographic addictions, past trauma, or even from a fear that sex is somehow shameful, the bedroom can seem so serious. Connecting intimately both physically and spiritually can take years for a couple to perfect. That's why sometimes it's important simply to chill.

If you've been married for a short time, or if you're about to tie the knot, accept that sex is probably the main area you'll devote emotional and physical energy to in the first few years of marriage. Any problems will seem huge because you both expected sex to go like clockwork, and it likely won't. You have two options when roadblocks pop up: you can sulk and blame, or you can throw up your hands, laugh, and say, "I guess it's going to take a while to get this right!" I did the first. I so wish I had done the second. And so, my dear sisters, in this chapter I'd like to show you how putting a high value on friendship and laughter lowers the stress in your marriage and smooths the way for a more fulfilling sex life.

> Sometimes it's important simply to chill.

Becoming Best Friends

Before we were married, my husband and I were once washing the dishes when I accidentally splashed him with water. He "accidentally" splashed me back. And within a few minutes a full-blown water fight had erupted, which I finally won because he was laughing too hard to fight back.

Couples who are close friends have fun together outside the bedroom, and that fun often feeds the more physical kind. You need to enjoy being together, to feel that the other person prioritizes your needs, and to feel as if you have something to share other than just genitals. Sex involves vulnerability, and we can't be vulnerable with someone we don't love and trust. We have to create that relationship first so the physical intimacy can then thrive.

Developing Common Hobbies

People may tell you that the main causes for divorce are money concerns, sex concerns, and problems with the kids. These are all important, but I think something far more fundamental is at work in all these issues: we don't connect. We've stopped being able to talk and solve problems, and the reason is usually quite simple: we've stopped doing life together. Two people can't solve problems if they don't first have a foundation of liking each other and laughing together. Before we can attack our marriage problems, we need to remember why we enjoy each other in the first place. We need to spend time together.

That's easier said than done because most of us don't share our spouse's hobbies. When we marry, guys settle into their hobbies, and we develop our own. Some couples soon find that the only things they do together are logistical: grocery shopping, errands, caring for children.

That's what happened to a couple who are very important to us—we'll call them Tanya and Mike. They were passionately in love when they married. Their physical attraction was solid, but unfortunately they had little else in common other than the children who came in quick succession. Early in their relationship they started to lead separate lives. Tanya stayed home with the children all day and then in the evening would occasionally convince Mike to watch them so she could go out for a girls' night. Mike drowned himself in video games. They didn't even eat together most nights since Mike would eat in front of the computer, and Tanya often ate with the kids. Not surprisingly, their marriage ended after less than a decade.

What is surprising is the number of couples who think this kind of distance is inevitable. Nonsense! Tanya and Mike did not have to drift apart; they could have drifted together if they had made an effort to stay connected.

And you and your spouse don't need to drift apart either. After all, you have a brain and a body. That means you can think and move. So figure out what you can do to move together! I hated gym class with such a passion that I used to fake asthma attacks to escape it. But that never meant I hated exercise; I just hated anything team oriented. So when my husband started playing squash with some friends, I decided it was worth a try. For five years, until our local squash club closed, we played squash several times a week. It helped us stay slim, and it was the impetus for loads of laughter.

Keith and I have taken ballroom dancing lessons too (though that took some prodding on my part). We've started cross-country skiing in the winter and biking in the summer. We have played board games with the children from the time they were old enough to graduate from Candy Land. We still have hobbies we do separately, but we also try to do some together.

Share His Interests

If you can't seem to find common ground with your husband, or if he doesn't sound enthusiastic about your new role as activities director, why not take an interest in what he already likes? If he enjoys hockey or football games, go with him occasionally. If he loves watching professional football, put some effort into learning about the teams and the rules and watch with him, even if you have to knit or crochet or cross-stitch at the same time.

My friend Lori took up hunting with her husband, and every

fall they head out to bag a deer together. Shooting Bambi may not be your idea of romance, but spending a weekend in a rustic hunting cabin, with only a wood stove for heat so you have to snuggle, can be a bonding experience.

Kendria and Juan had been married for twenty years when Kendria started to feel antsy. They had been active in their church, raised three great children, and led the youth. Gradually, though, Kendria confesses, they grew apart. Her life revolved around the kids, and his revolved around fishing and the gym. They had nothing in common anymore. When Kendria entertained thoughts of leaving, she panicked and took matters into her own hands. She explains:

> Last March our marriage suffered a huge blow. It was not looking good for us. Our church was having their annual fishing tournament, so I decided to go this year for the entire week and fish with my husband. I know it was the Lord! We purchased a boat, and in the four days on the boat and in the hotel, we really reconnected. And I won the tournament with a sixteen-pound catfish!
>
> I am surprised at how much I like to fish. I like the anticipation of the fish getting on my line. And I love the fight to bring the fish in the boat. I am surprised that I can and will bait my own hook! But I love the time we have to talk in between catching fish. It is so relaxing on the water. Now I understand why he loves it.
>
> My husband is proud of me for fishing. He brags all the time about my fishing skills. When we've gone into bait stores, I have heard at least ten men say, "Man, I wish my wife would fish with me!" I didn't understand how much just going fishing meant to my husband and other men.

Spending all day on a boat waiting for fish to bite while handling worms and fish guts wasn't something Kendria ever thought she'd enjoy. She and her husband were drifting apart, and she knew her marriage was in trouble. But look how that one relatively small thing—deciding to participate in his hobby—changed the whole dynamic of their relationship. Of course many guys pursue hobbies because they need their "man cave" time, or time just to be a guy without women around. Don't interfere with that time. But find a hobby you can share together, even if it isn't something you think you'd enjoy. You may just find your relationship is stronger for it.

When you spend time together and invest in each other's lives, navigating the bumps in a relationship becomes easier. The friendship you have built gives you strength to draw from. If all you ever do is iron his shirts or figure out who is picking up food tonight, problems will become magnified because you haven't developed a friendship.

Don't accept no for an answer in this realm of your life. You need to spend time doing something—almost anything—together regularly. It doesn't have to be strenuous. You can place a book you like reading aloud to each other on your bedside table. Keith and I have read Dave Barry's columns and humor novels to each other at night. When you laugh so hard you're afraid you might pee, you build memories and a great friendship!

Sharing Our Thoughts

Spending time together will make you feel more connected to your hubby, which will make you want to connect in other ways. But there's one more element we women need to get in the mood. We have to be able to share our thoughts and hearts too. Fast-forward ten years after the wedding, and the following scenario becomes all too frequent: It's been a long, hard day. You've wiped snotty noses, visited the bank and the dentist, and thrown food on the table before chauffeuring kids to karate. The principal called today and wanted to talk about a bullying incident having to do with your six-year-old. The karate club says that your eight-year-old has great potential and should take an extra lesson each week. And your sister called: she and her husband are having problems.

The kids are now in bed, and you want nothing more than to relax and let all those concerns fade away. You head into the bedroom, and there's your husband, whom you adore, getting ready for bed. But you know from the glint in his eye that sleep is not what he's planning.

You smile and scatter your clothes in all directions, following him to the bed, praying that the kids stay asleep and don't bug you. He reaches for you and starts kissing you. And then—from somewhere deep within, you're not even sure where—you find yourself pushing him aside and saying, "Do you think Jeffy should take two karate lessons a week? He is gifted, but I don't know if the teacher is just trying to get more money from us. And can we even swing it? When will we eat dinner as a family? But I know he really wants to do it. And then maybe he could teach his little brother to stick up for himself more when bullies pick on him. What do you think?"

Your husband sighs and rolls over as he grunts monosyllabic answers to your monologue about karate, bullies, money, dentists, and schedules.

Then, when you're finished, you start kissing him again, but he doesn't seem interested. You're mildly ticked at him for being ticked at you, but you can't quite put your finger on the problem. So you give him a peck on the cheek and roll over and go to sleep. *Maybe tomorrow night . . .*

Let's diagnose what's going on in this situation. Did you want to make love to your husband? Or were you pushing him away when you started talking?

From personal experience, here's my interpretation: you did want to make love, but you knew you weren't emotionally or mentally ready yet because you had to get out all the stuff in your head. As we've already learned, for women, sex is largely in our brains. If our heads aren't engaged, our bodies won't follow.

It took me awhile to figure that out about myself. I thought when I started talking instead of engaging in foreplay that I was somehow pushing my husband away. But I wasn't. My brain was trying to relieve itself of all the pressure so that I could be present with him. *Talking was the foreplay.* I wasn't looking for my husband to solve my problems; I needed to get out the concerns so that they weren't bouncing around in my brain like balls in a pinball game.

Now that Keith and I understand that need, our evenings look much different. We often take walks after dinner to talk about the pressures or frustrations I'm feeling so that they don't have to spill out right before bed. And Keith knows that for me that's part of warming up.

Maybe you're like that too. Explain to your husband that it's not that you don't want to make love but that you might not fully enjoy sex without that fifteen minutes of talking first to relieve the pressures of the day. Or maybe you need a fifteen-minute bubble bath just to unwind.

Sharing what's in your heart is a great start, but for most of us that's all it is: a start. We don't feel truly connected unless we also hear what is in our husbands' hearts. Unfortunately, men often aren't as interested in sharing feelings as women are; frequently they'd rather just share body parts. That doesn't mean they don't have feelings and thoughts to share, but some men are not comfortable discussing emotions. We women often value that face-to-face time. We like scrutinizing faces, watching laugh lines, and seeing ourselves reflected in their eyes. When we see eyeballs, we figure ears are listening. Without eyeballs, we figure we're being tuned out, right?

Not so fast! While women may like to communicate face-to-face, men often feel most comfortable and empowered communicating side by side. They're far more likely to open up and talk if they're doing something else at the same time, perhaps because it doesn't feel as vulnerable. So talk while you're walking, fishing, cooking, or driving. Don't demand that he sit across the table or bed from you and do nothing but talk for half an hour. That's likely not how he's made to share. Kendria, for instance, found that she and Juan hardly ever talked. But get her in that fishing boat, and suddenly he opened up!

Once you've developed that combination of spending time, sharing thoughts, and having fun, you'll likely find you're both far more receptive to spending more active time together at night. But sometimes cultivating that vital friendship isn't easy simply because life gets in the way. Let's look at common roadblocks to friendship.

Defeating Exhaustion

In 2010 a National Sleep Foundation Survey reported that 25 percent of people living with a spouse or partner reported being too tired to have sex.[2] I'm surprised that the number isn't higher. I remember when my daughters were little and I was so desperate to get at least six hours a night (even if it was broken up) that sex was far down on my priority list. It didn't mean that Keith and I weren't intimate, but I was far more attuned to my need for sleep than I was my need for sex.

> We may not think of exhaustion as a marriage issue, but it is.

Whether because of children or work or school or just life, many of us are run so ragged that sleep looks awfully appealing at night. Given the responses to my survey about sex, I think more women have rotten sex lives because they're too tired than because their husbands are distant. Exhaustion is our main problem. We may not think of exhaustion as a marriage issue, but it is. When we're tired, we don't have time to pay attention to our husbands because we're so desperate for time on our own to relax or rest.

Recharging Your Batteries

So let's treat exhaustion seriously. What drains your batteries? Your job, talking to certain people, doing housework, running after kids, chauffeuring, scheduling? Minimize those as much as possible. Stop calling your sister so much if she drives you crazy. Organize your errands and chores so they don't eat up as much time. And talk with your husband honestly if you're bearing too much of the load.

One of the biggest sources of mental and emotional exhaustion is mental load, as Eve Rodsky explains in her book *Fair Play*: "The never-ending mental to-do list you keep for all your family tasks. Though not as heavy as a bag of rocks, the constant details banging around in your mind nonetheless weigh you down. Mental 'overload' creates stress, fatigue, and often forgetfulness."[3] If your head is filled with swirling details you need to remember for everyone in the family, there may not be room for desire to build. Talk to your husband about a more equitable sharing of the mental load for the family so that you can have some headspace to get excited about sex.

Of course we can't eradicate everything that drains us. Toilets still need to be cleaned. Homework still needs to be supervised. Work still needs to get done. If you can't eliminate what makes you tired, add more of what gives you energy.

Don't always let yourself come last in your list of priorities. Schedule time during the day to rejuvenate. Often we feel physically exhausted when the actual problem is that we have too much on our plates and thus too much constantly going through our brains. Turn off the constant noise in your brain telling you to do more, and listen to the part of your brain telling you to slow down. You'll probably find you're less tired and more in the mood than when you're always focusing on everything you "should" be doing.

One of the biggest "shoulds" in your life is about your marriage. You *should* be enjoying your husband. Are you? If you're too tired to enjoy him, then you have to cut out activities and spend more time nurturing yourself. Growing your marriage should be a vital priority, but that means allowing yourself the mental and physical space to do so.

Random Acts of Kindness

When we're exhausted, we naturally think most of our own needs. We're depleted, and we need to be filled up. Thinking that someone else may need something from us is the last thing we want to hear. But that mentality often makes marriage worse.

Five years into our marriage our baby boy passed away. Keith and I felt God carrying us through that time, but it took years until we were back on our feet and could laugh and smile and live large. During that dark time, a wise woman advised us to write down twenty things that our spouse could do for us that would make us happy. The rules were simple: the things had to be easy to do, they had to be free (or at least cheap), and they had to have nothing to do with sex.

Coming up with twenty was a challenge, but we did it. They were small, like "Kiss me as soon as I come in the door," "Give me a neck massage," or "Let me overhear you tell a friend that you love me." None of them took an inordinate amount of effort, but they all made us feel loved.

Then we switched lists, and we had to commit to doing two or three things on that list a day. It became like a game: which ones could we carry out next? And it forced us to come out of our own headspace and enter into each other's. It made us realize that each one of us had needs.

We all have different love languages, and it was important for each of us to figure out how to make the other person feel cherished.[4] But more than figuring out what each other's love language was, we had to know what acts of kindness fit in with each of those love languages.

When we feel close to each other, these acts are easy to do. When we walk through a bleak time because of grief, busyness, illness, unemployment, or infertility, these gestures become harder because we tend to retreat into ourselves. Then we get angry because our spouse isn't meeting our needs—though any outside observer would instantly recognize that we're not exactly meeting his either. It's in those difficult times that it's even more important to challenge yourself to do acts of kindness. As we "act" kind, we tend to feel more tenderhearted and kindlier toward our beloveds too.

If you think doing acts of kindness is hard when you're exhausted, wait until you have children! Then a whole new level of stress conspires to rob you of your connection.

Putting the Marriage before the Kids

Pretty much every stage of parenthood provides its challenges: getting pregnant, being pregnant, caring for a baby, training a toddler, raising a teen, becoming an empty nester. Parenthood is busy and all-consuming, even when you're in the "just trying to get pregnant" stage, or perhaps even "trying *not* to get pregnant" stage. Birth control can put a damper on connection, since there isn't a perfect solution that allows total freedom but also doesn't kill libido. On the other hand, if you're trying to get pregnant, sex can lose its appeal too. It becomes all about ovulation. He doesn't like performing on a schedule, and you want him to hurry up and do it so you can conceive.

The timing and size of your family are important issues, and unless you feed your friendship, getting on the same page can prove awfully difficult. So keep talking, keep praying, and above all, keep working on having fun outside the bedroom. The more goodwill you build up in your relationship, the easier it will be to work through these difficult decisions and trying stages in your marriage.

All-Consuming Babies

As much of a challenge as preparenthood days are, parenthood can add a whole new layer of distance between you and your spouse.

When a baby comes, Mom automatically becomes preoccupied with the baby—and understandably so. She loses massive amounts of sleep—up to two months' worth in the first year of each baby's life, according to one British study.[5] And naturally her husband falls far down her priority list.

Part of this shuffling of priorities is natural to us women—we develop a strong physical bond with another human being who is always hanging off of us. We get our cuddle time from a baby, so we don't need it from our husbands as much. But don't give in to this tendency to retreat from your marriage. Your relationship with your husband is the foundational one in your family. Your husband was there first and will be there when the kids leave. And children fare best when their parents have a rock-solid relationship. *Do not let children displace your husband.* Yes, your kids will take most of your energy and most of your time, and their needs take precedence. But it's your relationship with your husband that will give you the energy to be the best mom you can be!

> Your relationship with your husband is the foundational one in your family.

Keep Your Bedroom to Yourself

Many parents opt for cosleeping, which means sleeping with the babies in bed (often called the "family bed" in parenting literature), because it helps Mom get more sleep (since she can breastfeed while lying there), and they feel it builds intimacy and bonding.

In my husband's pediatric practice, he often talks to couples who cosleep, and almost inevitably he finds that it is the wife's choice, not the husband's. The husband goes along with it because he feels like he must, but he's scared of rolling on the baby (a fear that is justified, as the American Academy of Pediatrics states[6]), and he doesn't like the new arrangement because he feels displaced.

When I asked about cosleeping on my Facebook page, I received dozens of answers from women, many of whom said something like this: "In your first year with a new baby, you're not going to sleep or have sex much regardless of where the baby sleeps. It's the lack of sleep that does it to you, not where the baby is. So bring the baby in bed if it helps you!"

Certainly in those first few months sleep is the main issue, and if Mama's tired, nothing's happening anyway. If cosleeping helps you sleep, then go ahead, providing you have read and accept the American Academy of Pediatrics' warning. But think twice before you make it a habit to invite older babies and toddlers to share your bed perpetually. You need a place where you and your husband can be "just the two of you." Having kids in your bed will kill your sex life. As one Facebook follower admitted, "Kids were our birth control." A proponent of cosleeping once told me that you could still keep your sex life alive, no problem: simply have silent, almost motionless sex! Can you imagine telling your husband, "Don't worry, honey, for the next few years we'll just have silent, motionless sex!" I can't think of many guys who would be enthralled with that.

Then there are the guys who feel as if their child has displaced them altogether, because Mom has either kicked him out of the bed so she can sleep with the kids, or has decided to go sleep in the kids' bedroom herself. Recently a husband wrote to me, "Ever since our two-year-old was born, my wife has been sleeping with him. She claims, 'It is so much easier to breastfeed him when I am next to him.' This has been going on for twenty-eight months. She now sleeps in the same room with our toddler and our baby. We have not slept in the same bed for well over two years."

Now, if you're sleeping in another room with the children instead of with your husband, it could be that your marriage is facing more serious issues than just sleep, and those issues should be addressed, ideally with a licensed counselor. But often we drift into cosleeping when babies are small and set up habits that are hard to break later. And sleeping away from your husband, or having children in between you and your husband on a semi-permanent basis, will impact your marriage. And that needs to matter. Parenting means that you have even more of a responsibility to work on your marriage, not less, because now more people depend on you.

Yes, you love your children. Yes, you want to comfort them. These are both good instincts! But your relationship with your husband is still the primary one, and that includes prioritizing sex. It's hard to do that if toddlers are sleeping between you. Some women told me that they can make love in another room if the kids are in bed, but I doubt that results in the same frequency as when you're already lying beside each other. You're more likely to have sex if you don't have to work as hard at it, so don't put up barriers to intimacy with your husband.

When Kids Grow

The roadblocks to intimacy don't end when babies are out of the bed; even when they grow, kids can put a damper on your sex life. Here's a busy woman, married for fourteen years, who says, "With four young kids and homeschooling, it is hard to feel like 'doing it.' We do talk once in a while to have him take some load off of my plate and try to prioritize couple time. We know that it takes work. I should initiate more often; I just don't have the energy at the end of the day."

Today this couple makes love less than once a week because she is so tired. Ironically, great sex might cure a lot of that tiredness (as might sharing more of the load with your husband)! When we make love, we release hormones into our bodies that relax us, and we sleep better. We feel more connected to our husbands, so we don't carry around guilt that we're disappointing them—guilt that is, in and of itself, exhausting.

Life is so busy that you can always find reasons for putting off sex. Don't accept them as excuses. When you see yourself falling into a rut of exhaustion, overcommitment, or worry, turn to your husband more, not less. Don't live in survival mode.

Keep Everything in Perspective

Couples often have highs and lows in their sex lives. Sometimes you'll have the higher sex drive, and sometimes he will. Rarely does your sex life have the same frequency, the same intensity, and the same physical rush for decades. Yet those who have a strong friendship find these ups and downs much easier to navigate. When you're friends, sex drives return faster. You want to give to each other. And when problems pop up, addressing them head-on is easier when the stress level in your marriage is already low.

So make this promise to yourself: *even if we go through a sexual rut, and even if I don't always feel attracted to him, I will do my best to increase the fun in our relationship.* Commit to finding new ways of laughing together and sharing together, and problems you have in the bedroom will diminish. And when sex doesn't go as you hoped, tell him, "Let's laugh about it and keep trying because we have years to improve!"

And while you're at it, order Chinese.

Part 3

THE JOURNEY
TO GREAT SEX

CHAPTER 8

From Fizzle to Sizzle for Her

I love the movie *The Notebook*, even if it does romanticize sex before marriage. If I could have my wish, I would ask God to take Keith and me together, wrapped in each other's arms, the way Noah and Allie left this earth.

But movies like this can also send us into spasms of self-loathing if sex doesn't work for us the way it worked for them. Everything went perfectly for that couple from the first time they made love, even though she was inexperienced. We wonder, "Why can't it work for me? What's wrong with me?"

Probably nothing. *The Notebook*, after all, is a movie, and movies rarely bear much resemblance to real life. (How many of us wake up in the morning and kiss our husbands deeply with no thought of morning breath?) Nevertheless, we tend to assume that sex will be like that famous *Notebook* scene. We will fall into bed and collapse into each other's arms in ecstasy, and each time thereafter will be a glorious encounter. Life doesn't work like that.

We've now covered the three aspects of intimacy that God designed for us to experience during sex. But what happens if, despite your best efforts and most fervent dreams and prayers, sex isn't turning out as you've hoped? We've looked at how sex is supposed to work. Now let's see what to do if a wrench is thrown into the mix.

Most couples experience physical issues with sex at some point, especially with pregnancy, the postpartum phase, or menopause. If you're in a marriage where everything worked like clockwork right off the bat, though, this chapter may not be necessary for you (though it's a good idea to know about these issues so you can give good advice to friends who may be struggling!). If you are having difficulties, here are some strategies to deal with the more common physical issues that arise.

I Don't Get Very Wet

Lubrication is essential for sex to feel good for women because dry skin rubbing against dry skin is not that nice. Think of the difference between having a massage when you have oil all over your back and having a massage with rough hands and no oil. No comparison.

But we produce lubrication only if our hormones are in the right balance (menopause, for instance, just about kills lubrication in many women). Women also have normal fluctuations throughout the month when it's easier to get "wet." Right around ovulation tends to be a wetter time, while right after your period tends to be a relatively dry time when you might have to spend more time warming up to become lubricated. You may feel mentally all raring to go, but your body may not make it as obvious. That can make your husband wonder if you're excited.

One man told us this:

> I used to think my wife was faking. She'd act all excited and would tell me she wanted me to start intercourse, but she'd barely be wet. But we've realized that over the course of the month, her lubrication really changes. She's often really into it mentally, but she just doesn't get that lubricated. She still reaches orgasm,

though! I've learned to trust what she says more than her lubrication level, and she's promised me she won't ever pretend she's into it when she's not.

If lubrication is hit-or-miss, devote enough time to getting yourself relaxed and turned on before you start intercourse. Take a shower together. Ask him to massage your back (just don't fall asleep!). Draw out foreplay so that you're relaxed, and tell him why that's important. No matter what the time of the month, if you're not relaxed, lubrication isn't likely.

If all that fails, there is an easy solution, and it's usually fewer than ten bucks. Simply head down to the drugstore, and go to the area where they sell condoms. Somewhere around there you'll find products called "personal lubricants." Once you try one, you'll likely find that it's much easier to get aroused.

It Hurts!

Piper and John had done everything right. They had aimed to save sex for marriage, and they made it all the way to their wedding night. The few big make-out sessions they'd enjoyed before marriage were often followed by feelings of intense guilt on Piper's part, and she would declare a fast from kissing for forty days. Yet even Piper was counting down the days until their wedding—and their wedding night.

After the dancing and the speeches and the confetti, they ended up in their hotel room, feeling awkward. They kissed a bit. They took off their clothes. But when they tried to have intercourse, they couldn't. Piper was so tense and so tight that it hurt too much.

It took the couple four years before penetration was possible—four years of trying and failing, four years of frustration and tears. They used other ways to bring John to orgasm, though Piper could never quite let John help her.

A few years into this struggle, Piper started seeing a physiotherapist who specialized in pelvic floor issues. She learned exercises to do to help her stretch and relax. Finally, after a lot of effort, penetration was possible, and they had their first child. But those years of frustration left their toll on the couple.

Their story is not unique. Our survey found that 22.6 percent of women had experienced vaginismus or other conditions that make intercourse painful (such as vulvodynia or lichen sclerosus), and 6.8 percent of women have had such bad sexual pain that penetration was impossible. Vaginismus, the most common sexual pain disorder, is caused when the muscles of the vagina tense up *involuntarily*.

Vaginismus was a large part of the early years of my marriage too. In my case, it wasn't so severe that penetration was impossible, but it was extremely painful. But I likely should have considered penetration "impossible" rather than pushing forward. When we were first married, few people had heard of pelvic floor physiotherapists. Instead, I was sent to psychiatrists and counselors who treated this problem like I had caused it, or as if I had some long-forgotten abuse in my past. We were led to believe that at some level I was rejecting sex with Keith psychologically and it was showing up in my body physically. You can imagine how much more guilty this made me feel!

Vaginismus, or sexual pain, isn't something that women deliberately cause. It doesn't mean you're psychologically scarred. It seems to be a multifaceted issue that can be impacted by stress, bowel issues, posture—basically anything that affects the pelvic floor. But it also seems to have some roots in beliefs we grow up with, because researchers have known for a long time that being religiously conservative is a risk factor for vaginismus. In our surveys, we tried to pinpoint what it was about being religiously conservative that contributed to sexual pain, and we found several markers. One was the obligation sex message: wives who believe before they are married that they are obligated to give their husband sex when he wants it are 37 percent more likely to experience vaginismus.

Another predictor of vaginismus is how the first sexual experience plays out. If women have had sex only with their now-husband, they are 25 percent more likely to have primary sexual pain if their first consensual sexual experience was on or after the wedding night.[1] Why? We think it has everything to do with arousal. Women who have sex on their wedding night aren't always aroused when it happens. But if they have sex before marriage? We believe women are much more likely to be aroused and *want* sex. We're not arguing for sex before marriage; only that this evidence gives us even more indication that it's vitally important not to rush through to intercourse as soon as you have that wedding ring on. Instead, work through the natural sexual progression to make sure you're aroused first (more on the honeymoon in the appendix!).

How to Treat Sexual Pain

For women with mild pain, learning some basic exercises to control those muscles can often fix the problem. Here's how: When you're peeing, try to stop the flow of urine. Feel those muscles? Those are the same ones that tense up when you have pain during sex. Try to tense and relax, tense and relax, three or four times until your body learns how to relax itself. Then, when you make love, have him enter you just a little way until it starts to hurt, and try the same thing: tense first, then relax. You may have to spend a few minutes doing this (try to treat it like a game, and for him it will probably feel pleasurable because you're squeezing him), and eventually you'll likely find that it doesn't hurt as much.

If you've tried this and still experience pain (or if you have a health plan and can afford it), a pelvic floor physiotherapist plays a large part in many women's recovery process for vaginismus. A pelvic floor physiotherapist will likely do some stretching exercises with you, give you exercises to do at home, and give a set of vaginal trainers (previously called dilators) that help you slowly stretch. This sounds horribly clinical, but it's just another way of saying "putting increasingly larger things in there," building up to something that is about the thickness of an erect penis.

When my friend Debbie was married, she was afraid she'd have issues because she had never been able to use tampons, and she had been sexually abused as a child. Sure enough, she found sex very difficult. Her husband was extremely patient with her, taking time to play around with her and allowing them both to be more relaxed. After four months, she found that the pain had gone away because she felt so accepted and loved. If sex hurts, tell your husband that story. Sure, it's hard to be patient. But his being patient will often help you to relax and release your real sexuality.

One more thought: communicate to your husband that you dream of a great sex life. If he knows that this is still your goal— even if you don't know how you'll get there—being patient will be much easier for him than if he thinks you're resigned to staying this way for the rest of your life.

While you work through sexual pain, give yourself a break. Don't feel guilty that you're depriving your husband of something he needs—remember that sex is just as much for you. Working through this struggle helps *both* of you, and you are not doing anything wrong by focusing on your recovery because you didn't do anything to cause this pain. Letting go of any toxic beliefs about sex that you may have brought into marriage can be helpful, and my book *The Great Sex Rescue* can help with that. But while you work on lessening the pain, focus on fun ways to connect sexually other than only intercourse. Let your husband help bring you to orgasm, and see what fun you can bring him too.

Let's Talk Pregnancy

We know that sex for women depends on our brains. We have to concentrate to enjoy it. Well, it's hard to concentrate if you feel like you're going to throw up, which is one of the reasons that pregnancy can wreak havoc on your sex life. If nausea doesn't flatten you, it could be the extreme fatigue in the first few months or the kicking in the later months or the discomfort of being so huge. If you become pregnant soon after you marry—or if you marry already being pregnant—then your sex life will be more challenging right from the beginning.

But here's some good news: many women find that pregnancy hormones increase their sex drives. The second trimester, between months four and six, can often be a sexually exciting time. One of my friends who has numerous children reports that she often has to wake her husband up at 5:30 a.m. in those middle months because she's so turned on. Pregnancy does not have to be all bad news for your sex life.

But what do you do if you're busy puking and dreaming of nothing but sleep and food you can keep down? It may be that your sex life will take a dive in those first few months, but try to compensate by doing a lot of touching and massaging or taking baths or showers together, which can help you feel better.

And what if you do want to try sex? *It won't hurt the baby.* Honest. If you're having bleeding and the doctor tells you to refrain, that's one thing, but in the vast majority of healthy pregnancies, sex doesn't hurt the child at all. Later in your pregnancy, you may find that positions other than the standard "missionary" are more comfortable. Many women enjoy being on top, since lying on one's back becomes impossible. "Spooning," with you both lying on your sides, him behind you, can also work. Then he can also reach around and stimulate your clitoris at the same time, even if it can be a bit of trial and error of pregnancy gymnastics to make the position work.

The added benefit of sex is that it can bring on labor, so if you feel like a beached whale at your due date and baby doesn't seem eager to emerge, why not try it? It just may benefit all three of you!

Challenges That Come with the Postpartum Phase

When I gave birth to Rebecca, my firstborn, I had such a bad tear that I couldn't walk for six weeks. It took me much longer to recover from childbirth than it takes most women. When Rebecca had her firstborn, she had even more problems than I did.

Some women have easy births and they're good to go even before the six-week checkup (though you should wait until the doctor gives you the go-ahead). But six weeks isn't a magic number at which all healing is done. Some women's bodies experience more trauma, some newborns sleep much worse than others, and some moms go through postpartum depression. We have to give ourselves grace in those days and go at the pace of our own bodies. Our study found that 26.7 percent of women experienced significant postpartum pain with sex. For some women, vaginismus can develop after childbirth, either exacerbated by new scar tissue or from a traumatic birth experience. Again, the go-to treatment for sexual pain is with a pelvic floor physiotherapist. With treatment and time, most women recover.

But if you push sex too early when it's painful, you may exacerbate your postpartum problems while creating a whole host of new ones. If you believe you must have sex for his sake, despite your own pain, that creates an ugly narrative in your mind about sex. Feeling like the way that he feels loved is by doing something that causes you pain is a traumatic message. Love does not require someone else's pain. Listen to this anguished woman's words:

> My husband and I used to enjoy sexual intimacy and never had any problems—until after the birth of our first child. When we tried intercourse, it was extremely painful. We have unsuccessfully tried several times since then. The sexual dysfunction exposed underlying issues in our relationship that we have not been able to repair, and we are heading toward separation. My husband has a very fundamentalistic view of the Bible, and I

think he would like me to suffer through the pain and fulfill my duty for his sake. That duty mentality completely kills any arousal and does not help fix my problem of pain. I just can't do it. That's not to say I am not open to other ways of being sexually intimate, it is just that this hostility between us makes it seem impossible to do with a sincere heart.

It is interesting to me that when it is my body that got injured during birth (pelvic organ prolapse) and my body that now experiences pain during intercourse, he acts as if he is the only one hurting. I know he loves me, but I feel so objectified. The fact that my husband wants me to have sex with him despite intense pain disgusts me, and I really question who I chose to marry.

If your husband is pushing you to have intercourse when it is painful, this is a sign that you are not in a healthy marriage and could even be in an abusive one. You do not have to tolerate being abused. Please seek qualified help.[2]

Pain is not the only issue with postpartum sex. You may also start leaking in all new ways! When women are aroused, we can stimulate milk production. In fact, orgasm can prompt the "let down" reflex, and many women find themselves squirting when they don't want to. If you produce a lot of breast milk, having sex while wearing a bra and nipple pads, or with a towel across your chest and under your back, can make everything less messy.

I'm Never in the Mood!

In one of the surveys I conducted leading up to this book, 29 percent of women reported that they believed they had a lower sex drive than most women (though how they would judge this is difficult to say!). But *low* is a relative term. Many women report having a low sex drive when really it's only that it's lower than their husband's. He wants sex every day—or several times a day—and she's

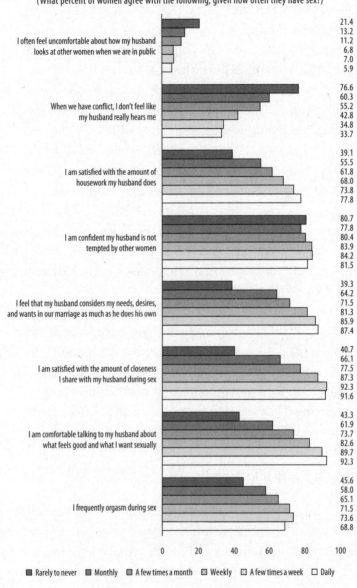

What is the effect of sex frequency on women's marital and sexual satisfaction?
(What percent of women agree with the following, given how often they have sex?)

I often feel uncomfortable about how my husband looks at other women when we are in public
- 21.4
- 13.2
- 11.2
- 6.8
- 7.0
- 5.9

When we have conflict, I don't feel like my husband really hears me
- 76.6
- 60.3
- 55.2
- 42.8
- 34.8
- 33.7

I am satisfied with the amount of housework my husband does
- 39.1
- 55.5
- 61.8
- 68.0
- 73.8
- 77.8

I am confident my husband is not tempted by other women
- 80.7
- 77.8
- 80.4
- 83.9
- 84.2
- 81.5

I feel that my husband considers my needs, desires, and wants in our marriage as much as he does his own
- 39.3
- 64.2
- 71.5
- 81.3
- 85.9
- 87.4

I am satisfied with the amount of closeness I share with my husband during sex
- 40.7
- 66.1
- 77.5
- 87.3
- 92.3
- 91.6

I am comfortable talking to my husband about what feels good and what I want sexually
- 43.3
- 61.9
- 73.7
- 82.6
- 89.7
- 92.3

I frequently orgasm during sex
- 45.6
- 58.0
- 65.1
- 71.5
- 73.6
- 68.8

0   20   40   60   80   100

■ Rarely to never ■ Monthly ■ A few times a month ☐ Weekly ☐ A few times a week ☐ Daily

content with a few times a week or even once a week. That's not a low sex drive; that's simply a discrepancy between sex drives. She's perfectly normal.

And how is "normal" defined? Truly low libidos are associated more with difficulties becoming aroused than they are with not wanting sex very often. If you're doing everything right but don't find your body responding and you rarely think about sex, even in your dreams, then you very well may have a low libido. We'll address normal libido issues in a later chapter, but let's turn here to women whose sex drives seem to have disappeared.

If you never think about sex or dream about sex, ask for your hormone levels to be tested. A whole cocktail of hormones contributes to women's libido, including testosterone, estrogen, progesterone, and more. When they're out of balance, libido can be affected. Menopause and perimenopause, when hormone levels change quickly, can also cause havoc on libido. Some hormonal creams, applied to the genitals, can work wonders.

Other medical conditions can also contribute to low libido, like diabetes and thyroid disease, so talk to your doctor to rule out serious health issues. Depression and other mental health issues, and often the medications used to treat them, can also send your libido through the floor. Hormonal birth control can eliminate those libido surges we often have in the middle of the cycle. If you feel that something may be hindering your sex drive, speak to a physician because often conditions have treatments, or medications that disrupt libido can be substituted with ones that do not.

Finally, for many women the hormonal changes from menopause wipe out what was once a healthy libido. Not all women experience worse sex after menopause, but many do. Hormonal treatments, better diet, more exercise, and using lubricants can help with libido and sexual arousal. Increased blood flow to the genitals causes much of physical arousal, but menopause brings with it less blood flow to that area and less lubrication. Spend more time warming up and relaxing, use lubricants or even vaginal suppositories to fight against dryness (you can even get flavored ones!), and take your time. If you find that your ability to orgasm has disappeared, talk to your physician or health care provider about treatment options. As Dr. Carol Peters-Tanksley, an ob-gyn and author of *Dr. Carol's Guide to Women's Health* told me, orgasm can become harder after menopause, but there's no medical reason why you can't orgasm at all. She elaborated, "The orgasmic peak post-menopausal women experience may not feel quite as dramatic as in earlier years, but it can be intensely satisfying. If there's one encouragement I have for postmenopausal women when it comes to sex, it's SLOW DOWN! Longer foreplay, more conscious attention to what feels good, alternating between lighter and more intense stimulation—you've earned the right to take the time and enjoy it! You have every reason to continue to enjoy orgasmic sex for as many years as you wish."[3]

Embracing Sex When You Feel Awful

I recently received an email from a woman married ten years who was in a difficult spot. She suffered from chronic pain, which made sex very difficult, so she preferred not to have it at all. Her husband didn't think he could live like that.

At times in your relationship, whether it's due to pregnancy, hormones, or health concerns, sex may become painful or difficult. That leads to the unfortunate dynamic where your husband wants pleasure from something that causes you pain.

I want to be clear here: you never have to do something that causes you pain. He should not get pleasure from your discomfort. That isn't right. But at the same time, sometimes the situation seems bleaker than it is.

Since women's sex drives are largely in our heads, for us to become aroused, our heads have to be engaged. But we are extremely distractible. If a stray thought comes into our heads, we can lose any amount of arousal we feel. Thus, something as simple and common as a headache is a real roadblock for most women. When we feel the intrusion of pain, getting in the mood is supremely hard.

Yet sex is often the best treatment. Researchers have found that orgasm is one of the best cures for migraines.[4] The sudden release and euphoria often stop the pain. Frequent sex even seems to prevent migraines. So even though it's counterintuitive, sex often helps with headaches (as long as you reach orgasm). The same is true for muscle pain. Sex allows muscles to relax, giving a tremendous physical boost. And it helps us sleep much better!

I know it's hard to see sex as a cure when you're in pain, but for some people it may be. Talk to your doctor to see whether sex might help you. The key is to get to the point where you can physically enjoy sex even when your body itself is in great discomfort and very tense. It may be that you need to spend a lot of time relaxing first, in a hot bath with your spouse or with a massage. You may need to work at finding a position that feels comfortable for you. You may even need to work at achieving orgasm some other way than intercourse, since it's orgasm that helps you relax. Simply having intercourse without orgasm is unlikely to help alleviate much of anything.

Explain to your husband that you do love him and cherish him and want your marriage to be great but that you're really down and exhausted by this pain. Tell him you want to connect physically and sexually so that you feel better together and also so that your body finds new ways to relax and get some sleep. That means sex, for you, has to be gentle, drawn out, and low pressure. He'll have to become awesome at foreplay, especially massage. But the good part is that you can connect more and feel more intimate. And ultimately, that's what sex was created for.

CHAPTER 9

From Fizzle to Sizzle for Him

When our daughters were six and four, we treated them to a day at the zoo. They loved the orangutans, penguins, and polar bears. But when we hit the Japanese macaque exhibit, Keith and I froze in our tracks. All around us, parents were shielding kids' eyes from these large monkeys. For there, for all to see, was one very large male macaque humping every female in sight. He'd launch onto one, thrust a few times, then grab another for good measure.

"Look, Mommy!" Rebecca exclaimed. "He's playing horsey! The monkey is playing horsey!" She talked about that randy monkey all through the zoo that day, and as we exited, she announced to the smiling attendant, "We saw monkeys playing horsey!" The woman shot a knowing glance our way.

Our culture's conception of male sexuality is that every guy would secretly, or even not so secretly, like to be that male macaque, humping all the time—though we hope he'd settle for only one partner rather than four. But what if your guy isn't that into sex?

Male sexual dysfunction gets weeded out in the rest of the animal kingdom, but it finds rather effective breeding grounds in modern marriages. Health problems, relationship issues, and stress can all hinder a man's ability to perform sexually. And when things go wrong in the bedroom, men often panic even more than women do because their self-esteem is often closely related to their sexual prowess. Panic, though, almost always makes it worse. When things aren't working for him, here are some specific strategies to relax and rebuild your physical lives.

Erectile Dysfunction

Erectile dysfunction (ED) is the most common problem men face in the bedroom. A multinational study of men ages twenty to seventy-five found an overall incidence of 16 percent. It increases with age, from 8 percent in men twenty to thirty, up to 37 percent in men over seventy.[1] As men age it often takes more direct stimulation to produce an erection and to keep one, let alone to reach orgasm. For many men, this is a benefit—they find they can make sex last longer than when they were twenty-three and desperate. It's also part of the reason why older men are labeled better lovers—they're able to last longer. But when they can't perform at all, then ED becomes a problem.

Erections depend on good circulation, since blood flow is what causes the penis to grow hard. Anything that hinders circulation or decreases one's heart rate can lead to erectile dysfunction, including smoking and alcohol use, so encourage your husband to cut back if he wants to have more sex. The onset of erectile dysfunction can also be an indicator of possible coronary artery disease, even in men with few other risk factors. Diabetes, high blood pressure, and hypothyroidism are also strongly linked to erectile dysfunction. Men may hate going to the doctor, but if ED is chronic, it's worth having a checkup. In other cases, problems in the sexual organs themselves can cause ED. Many men recovering from prostate cancer, for instance, find ED a common side effect. Again, physicians can help with strategies to alleviate these problems or can suggest ways to achieve sexual fulfillment even if erections can't be maintained.

If you find that, due to health issues, ED becomes a chronic condition, it's okay to feel as if you have something to grieve. But you can still enjoy yourselves and stay connected even with ED. One woman, whose husband is in his sixties, wrote, "He is having prostate problems, and although he can still function, he is embarrassed, feels he isn't as much a man. In the past this might have been a big problem, but it's actually not bad now; we're actually growing closer in other ways because of it. Getting to be closer friends, etc. . . . . That's pretty cool."

This woman has a great attitude and a wonderful way of looking at the problem. When your husband's body stops working like clockwork, mourn what you've lost, but please keep celebrating what you still have.

Erectile dysfunction does not always have a physical cause. Instead, the problem may have a psychological or emotional root. Whether the culprit is challenges at work or worries about the relationship, the cause of ED can be related to a man's insecurity.[2] *Am I able to provide for the family? Does she still want to be here?* It also can strike around issues of fatherhood: men can develop ED during periods of infertility, and many others develop it after a child arrives—they're afraid of the added responsibility that babies bring. Others experience it during periods of unemployment.

In these cases, ED shouldn't initially be a cause for great concern because it will likely end as soon as the man feels better about himself. Take the focus off sex and put it on your relationship. And above all, don't contribute to the "impotence domino effect" that occurs when one night doesn't go well and he freaks out about it and questions his masculinity so much that it keeps recurring. When it does happen, laugh it off and tell him, "I know it will work tomorrow, so let's just do something else fun," and then watch a movie together. Don't dwell on it. Don't even talk about it too much. Certainly don't baby him! Treat him exactly as you normally would, and then try again a day or two later. But if it continues, encourage your husband to see his doctor or a licensed counselor to talk about any emotional or relational issues that may be contributing to the problem.

Porn-Induced Erectile Dysfunction

When we think of erectile dysfunction, we usually picture older guys in late-night commercials talking about little blue pills. But there's another face of erectile dysfunction that surprises many people: it's a guy in his twenties or thirties whose sexual response has been disrupted by pornography. And the little blue pill isn't the answer because it's not a circulatory problem. In younger men, sexual dysfunction is highly correlated with porn use. In my survey of guys, men who never use porn are 2.4 times less likely to have erectile dysfunction than men who use it daily. Porn trains his brain to become aroused by an image or video rather than relationship, and then when he's with you, you don't provide the right kind of excitement. One of the lures of porn, you see, is that it's always different. With an alcohol addiction, an alcoholic eventually develops tolerance; the same amount of alcohol doesn't give the same buzz, and so more is needed. With porn, it's not that he needs *more*; it's that he needs *different*—different bodies, different actions, different scenarios. That's why the type of porn users seek out often becomes more and more extreme. As the search for "different" and "new" intensifies, guys seek images that they initially would never have wanted to see.

As we talked about earlier, porn use cannot be tolerated. If your husband uses porn, please seek out a licensed counselor to talk about next steps, and make it clear that the porn use must stop.

Delayed Ejaculation

Delayed ejaculation—when men take an abnormally long time to reach orgasm, or never reach orgasm at all—can also mess with sexual satisfaction. Again, delayed ejaculation is highly linked to porn use. In our survey, men who use porn daily were 4.1 times more likely to have delayed ejaculation than men who never use porn. Because the sexual response cycle has been associated with pornography and masturbation, he may find it difficult to reach orgasm with less intense stimulation. Once men quit porn use, the problem usually takes care of itself with time.[3]

Porn is not always the issue with delayed ejaculation. There are other causes, including certain medications. In that case, encourage him to seek medical help.

Premature Ejaculation

Premature ejaculation occurs when a man orgasms faster than normal and faster than he or his wife would like. Doctors used to define premature ejaculation as ejaculation within a specific time frame—for example, men reaching orgasm before two minutes—but that has been thrown out since we now know that most men can reach orgasm that quickly if they try. Today it is defined as a lack of ejaculatory control that interferes with the sexual enjoyment of one or both partners. While the incidence of premature ejaculation does increase with porn use, the statistical effect is not nearly as great as with other forms of sexual dysfunction.

It's quite likely that most men, when first married, won't be able to stretch intercourse out beyond a few minutes before they climax, especially if they are sexually inexperienced. Sex is something new that's highly exciting. They haven't yet learned to control their body's reflexes. So don't start worrying about premature ejaculation until you've given your guy time to get used to sex!

Once you've been sexually active for a while together, he should be able to develop some strategies to delay orgasm. If sex continues to be over too quickly for you to enjoy it, don't start actual intercourse until you're already highly aroused. Spend a ton of time relaxing together and in foreplay so that by the time he enters you, you're almost ready to go. Another solution may be as simple as using thicker condoms. Other men have benefitted from using the pause-squeeze technique or the start-stop technique. Finally, there may be medications his doctor can prescribe if these techniques haven't worked.

––––– **TECHNIQUES TO HELP WITH PREMATURE EJACULATION**[4] –––––

The Pause-Squeeze Technique

- Engage in sexual activity until he is close to ejaculation.
- Stop and squeeze his penis firmly where the head joins the shaft until the urge to ejaculate passes and his erection starts to diminish. This should not be painful. If anything hurts him, stop immediately.
- Repeat as necessary. The point is to train him to recognize the signals in his body that occur before he reaches orgasm.

The Start-and-Stop Technique

- Engage in sexual activity until he is close to ejaculation.
- Stop once he feels he is close to orgasm.
- Wait until the urge to ejaculate passes, then resume.
- Repeat this three times with the goal of having an orgasm on the fourth time.
- Repeat as necessary. It can take weeks before you see a difference.

He's Never in the Mood!

One of the most common complaints readers email me about is husbands not wanting sex. A typical email says something like, "I am so sick of hearing women complain about how their husbands want it all the time. I just want my husband to want it *some* of the time!"

One forty-two-year-old woman, married for eighteen years, explains the rejection she feels this way:

> Because my husband does not want me sexually, I have a hard time believing him when he tells me how much he loves me. We have a friendship, a life together, but without sex and affection it feels like we are roommates more than anything else. I often feel very alone in this because so many women talk about how their husbands want sex more than they do. I'll just say that not being wanted feels awful.

Another twenty-three-year-old woman, married just a few months, echoed her thoughts:

> I expected my husband's drive to be stronger than mine, so when mine turned out to be stronger, I felt extremely unwanted. It has impacted the beginning of our marriage in a terrible way.

To make matters worse, many women who endure their husband's low sex drive are also greeted with jeers from their friends: "I wish my husband would give me a break sometimes!" That's hardly helpful when you're sexually frustrated or feel undesirable.

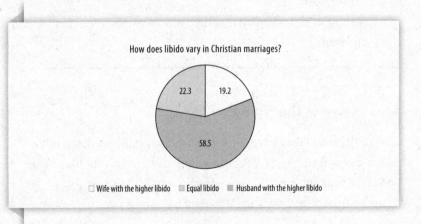

How does libido vary in Christian marriages?

22.3 19.2 58.5

☐ Wife with the higher libido ▨ Equal libido ▨ Husband with the higher libido

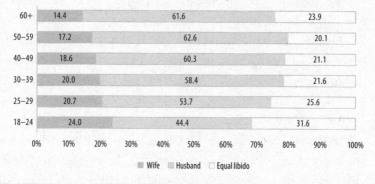

Libido Difference By Age

Age	Wife	Husband	Equal libido
60+	14.4	61.6	23.9
50–59	17.2	62.6	20.1
40–49	18.6	60.3	21.1
30–39	20.0	58.4	21.6
25–29	20.7	53.7	25.6
18–24	24.0	44.4	31.6

You may feel like a freak. Why does everyone else's husband want sex, and yours doesn't?

But you're not a freak. In the survey we conducted of twenty thousand women, we found that 19 percent of wives have the higher libido. And it varies with age too.

Now it's one thing if you want sex two or three times a week and he's more a once-a-week or once-every-ten-days guy. We'll be looking at how to bridge that gap in the next chapter. Here, though, let's look at what to do if your libido mismatch falls outside that normal range, leaving you desperate and frustrated.

Medical and Hormonal Conditions

About five million American men suffer from low levels of testosterone, the hormone responsible for sexual arousal. If your husband seems to have a low libido, encourage him to have it checked out. A simple blood test can verify whether he does indeed have low hormone levels. If nothing else is wrong (often there's an underlying disease causing low testosterone, which would have to be treated), low testosterone on its own can be corrected with hormone replacement therapy.[5]

One reader shared their success story: "In the past, my hubby had little to no sex drive. His doctor tested him for testosterone, and he was way low. Put him on meds, and wowza! He wants me as much as I want him."

Just like for women, many medical conditions like diabetes, heart disease, or thyroid conditions can affect libido, as can mood disorders and the medications used to treat them.

Porn and Addictions

Addiction to porn will lower his libido, but so will addiction to just about anything. If your husband spends hours every night with video games or streaming TV shows, he's not likely to want to make love often. When addiction affects a couple's sexual relationship, it needs to be dealt with. Ask him to seek out addiction recovery groups in your area. Remember, though, that you can't fix this for him. If he isn't willing to work on recovery, seek out a counselor yourself to learn how to set boundaries and deal with any betrayal and loneliness you feel.

Emotional Issues

Other men have trouble with libido because they're scared of sex itself. One thirty-two-year-old woman who reports having sex less than once a month explains that the problem is her husband's upbringing: "We're still trying to work through the damage done by his parents' fundamentalist teachings of sex, thus making him feel like sex is a bad thing."

Still others suffer from fear: fear they're not good in bed, fear that they're inadequate compared to your past lovers, or fear that they may experience erectile dysfunction. For these emotionally based fears, the best defense is building your friendship and the trust in your relationship so that he knows you accept him completely.

Stress can also affect libido, and if your husband is so stressed that his sex drive is gone, it may be time to reevaluate your priorities and your work goals and look at finding a simpler lifestyle. Unless you know the stress is short-term, like the final year of university with all the exams, or the first year of interning at a law firm, living with that level of stress is likely untenable.

Finally, some women are married to men who are genuinely asexual (they don't have any desire for sex at all) or have a different sexual orientation. He may honestly love you but not be sexually attracted to you because of his own sexual makeup, not because of anything wrong with you. If this is the case, please see a licensed counselor for help.

With Great Sex, Less Can Be More

Last year I taught at a retreat where I was also asked to do a breakout session on increasing our libidos. During the question-and-answer session, one bold woman put up her hand and asked, rather emphatically, "What do you do if your husband is just huge?" Since their wedding, her husband had gained over a hundred pounds. She found it difficult to look at him as she once did and think, "Ooh, baby, come and take me." Then there's also the simple physical issue of him being rather heavy. Excess weight does affect people's experience of sex. Yes, beauty is more than skin deep, but we also have to consider the simple biomechanics of how bodies fit together.

Because of the angle of penetration, a husband's obesity can make it more difficult for a wife to experience pleasure during intercourse. A large part of what feels good for her is having his pubic bone put pressure on her clitoris with every thrust. But excess weight in the belly region can prevent the clitoris from getting any stimulation during thrusting. As well, when a man is on the obese end of the spectrum, losing even a bit of weight can give him more usable penile length, harder erections, and more stamina so that sex is just plain better. Plus, there's the breathing factor! When there's a large discrepancy in weight between the husband and wife, sex in the man-on-top position can make it difficult to breathe, while sex in the woman-on-top position can cause strain on your legs and hips if you have to straddle too wide.

Now, bigger guys can be awesome lovers. They can learn to bring you to orgasm in different ways and learn how your body works and make you feel amazing. But his weight may make enjoying intercourse tricky.

As well, one of the biggest culprits in male low libido can be the amount of fat in their bodies. Fat cells produce estrogen, which works against testosterone—the libido builder—in men. The more estrogen, the less desire. Robert Rister, an author and chemist who has written at length on how to cure low libido naturally, says, "Nothing does more to restore male sex drive than achieving normal weight."[6] Losing weight boosts men's self-esteem because they feel physically better about themselves, and it cuts down on estrogen. And here's another tip: stay away from beer. Hops, the main ingredient in beer, acts similarly to the way estrogen does in your body. In the Middle Ages, monks used to make their teenage novices drink beer to quell sexual desire, reports Rister. Beer has even been linked to erectile dysfunction. Flee from hops, and the gut may go away too![7]

Now, what if it's *your* body that has expanded? Again, we need to focus on health and function and not appearance. No one should be expected to look the same way that they did on their wedding day. One male commenter on my blog once claimed that if a woman gains more than twenty-five pounds after her wedding that she's defrauding him and has broken her marriage vows! This view isn't okay, and if your husband requires you to stay a certain weight to find you attractive, that's a signal that something is emotionally wrong with your marriage, and is even abusive, so you should seek out a counselor. He has likely developed that "pornographic style of relating."[8] You should not feel objectified in your marriage; you should feel cherished.

No one is entitled to a spouse whose body looks the same as it did at twenty-one, and women have more natural reasons for our bodies to change than men do. Having babies means that your stomach will inevitably not be as tight as it was before. Your lower torso may always look like a highway map, with stretch marks zigzagging across. *Perky* may never be a word to describe your breasts again. And that needs to be okay. I wish everyone's husband had the attitude that one man did at a marriage conference we spoke at. When his wife worried that her postbaby body wasn't back to what it was, he told her, "You should be proud of your body; you worked hard for it!"

That being said, there is a distinct difference between typical weight gain (postpartum and with age) and weight gain that carries risks to health and that makes intercourse virtually impossible. Whether the issue is with you or your husband or with both of you, ignoring the problem won't help anybody. Just remember to address the issue in terms of health rather than appearance.

Our society tends to glorify the physical over everything else, and so the intimacy that we can feel from being close to someone we love is underrated. If the physical part of your marriage isn't exhilarating, maybe the companionship is. Focus on being emotionally intimate. Take walks together. Do things together. Laugh together. Play together. The more you spend time in each other's company cherishing each other, the more you will want to express that physically.

And then stress the companionship when making love. Look into his eyes. Remind yourself of what you love about him, what you find sweet about him, what makes him a great husband. Even if both of you have more to love, you're still *you*. And he's who you fell in love with too, and that's not changing.

Think outside the Box

The weekend marriage conference was wrapping up after the Saturday sex session, and people were grabbing their coats and leaving for dinner with eager smiles on their faces. As Keith and I walked over to our book table, a man in his late fifties came over to us, brimming with excitement. "Our sex life isn't over!" he announced.

We weren't sure what we had said that triggered this response, but he shared with us that a year and a half prior he'd had some major health issues that had rendered intercourse virtually impossible. They felt like they had lost a big part of their lives. But in listening to us talk about how sex is not just intercourse—how physically it can encompass much more, including being naked together and touching each other—he realized he had given up too soon. He had felt like their sex life was over since they couldn't have intercourse, and so he'd been avoiding being naked with his wife. Realizing that touching each other wasn't some cheap substitute for the real thing, but could be intimate and special too, opened up a future for him.

Let's not think of sex so narrowly that when physical problems take intercourse off the table, we assume we can't be sexual anymore. You can still cuddle naked. You can still massage each other. And chances are, you can still bring each other to orgasm in other ways. Even if your bodies don't work the same as they did when you first married, you can still nurture intimacy on all levels. Your husband isn't just the only one you have intercourse with; he's also the only one you lie naked in a bath with, massage naked, and touch all over. So let's embrace a wider definition of sex so we can enjoy it more—no matter what the future brings.

CHAPTER 10

The Sex Cycle

Learning to Give

When a woman walks down the aisle, she does so because she firmly feels that the man facing her, fighting back tears, is the man who will make her feel loved for the rest of her life. Their marriage will be a picture of love and passion.

But all too often, after she's been married for a few years, she doesn't necessarily feel very loved, and passion may never have blossomed. Sex, instead of being the beautiful experience I've been describing throughout this book, may seem like one more thing on her to-do list. And, quite frankly, she may be awfully tired of it.

Here's an email I received asking a question that occurs to many wives at some point:

> Where does it say that everyone's appetites will be filled? There are a lot of things I want or would like to have but no guarantees I can have them just because I want them. It would be nice if we all had equal appetites, sure. But when one isn't as interested (due to lack of drive, stress, etc., not withholding out of anger) why must they be the one who needs to fix their "problem"? . . . Why shouldn't the other be advised to control his or her urges?

Plenty of women feel that marriage would be much better if sex weren't a factor—if we could just snuggle and talk and be good friends, maybe while sharing a box of chocolates. Other women have the opposite problem: they understand that sex is supposed to be awesome, but for some reason their husband missed the memo. He's the one who never seems to want to.

Regardless of who has the higher libido, libido differences can cause not only conflict but also emotional distance. Both of you can feel unloved: one because the other doesn't want sex; the other because their spouse seems to want *only* sex. That was our story, and it was easy early in our marriage for me to feel like sex was the source of all our problems. Get rid of sex and we'd be great again!

But sex is a vital part of a healthy marriage relationship. God made it so that in sex we reaffirm our commitment and feel deeply bonded. In this chapter, I want to help navigate libido differences by showing two things: First, libido differences may not be the problem that we think they are. We might simply misunderstand what libido means. Second, committing to fostering libido is a way of showing love to both your husband *and* to yourself. And if he's the one with the lower libido? We'll look at how we can foster a marriage where both are more likely to feel wanted—including you.

What Is Libido, Anyway?

Libido is simply when your mind and emotions say, "I want sexy time!" It's less about your body's physical reactions and more about your emotional and mental attitude toward sex. Remember how I told you back in the physical section that we would return to the sexual response cycle later and add another element to it? Well, "later" has arrived, and it's time to add *desire*, or the mental component of libido, to our cycle.

For some people, the sexual response cycle looks like this:

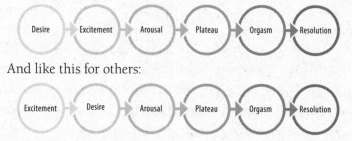

And like this for others:

Notice the difference? Some people experience *spontaneous* desire (often called "libido"), where they want to have sex and even start to become physically turned on *before they start physically doing anything.* Other people feel the desire for sex only after they've started touching each other and getting excited. That's what we'll call *responsive* desire.

We're going to talk in generalities here, and you may not fit these stereotypes (which is perfectly fine), but generally men tend to be in the first category (spontaneous libido), and women tend to be in the second (responsive libido). Men tend to be more visually stimulated, so sometimes they can see their wife and immediately jump through the desire phase to the excitement phase. (Research is now emerging saying that this may be largely cultural, and many women are very visually stimulated too.[1] And many women can also have spontaneous libidos, though in my surveys, men were about three times more likely to report this libido dynamic than women.) Many women, on the other hand, aren't turned on in the same way. They don't skip rapidly through desire into excitement simply by a look or a stray thought; they need to be physically warmed up first before desire even registers. And arousal? That doesn't tend to kick in until well after some of that warming up.

Television shows and movies often portray everybody as having the same sexual response cycle: They see their mate, they start panting, and they make love. If you're not panting, you might figure that you're not interested. It's easy to conclude that you're not a very sexual person.

But for many women the desire phase comes *after* the excitement phase. When our survey looked at women who are reliably aroused by the time sex is finished, we found that 70.9 percent of them aren't aroused when they start—but they know they'll get there! And women who are always aroused by the end of sex—whether or not they were aroused before all that touching started—reported very positive feelings about sex. So here's some reassurance for you: if you're not panting first, that doesn't mean you don't want sex or don't find your husband attractive; it means you have more of a responsive libido. For you, desire kicks in after some affection and fooling around. That's when your mind says, "Okay, sexy-sexy time now!"

If you're more of a responsive person, and you look at your spontaneous libido hubby, who started getting erections in seventh grade whenever some girl wore a tight sweater, it's easy to suspect that males are somehow the lesser species. We were created a little closer to the angels, and men were created a little closer to the lizards. We flourish on deep, important things, like emotional connection, while they focus on breasts. But having a spontaneous libido does not mean he's more "animal" and you're more "angel." You're both still built to be sexual. You simply approach it in different ways.

When we don't understand that responsive libidos *are still libidos*—that someone can be responsive and still be a sexual person—then we often assume that sex isn't for us. We're not made for it. It's something men need that we don't. And so it can be easy to let sex fall to the wayside. But then we're depriving our husbands—and ourselves!—of something amazing for no good reason. *There is nothing wrong with you if you don't have a spontaneous libido.* It means you're, well, in the majority. That's what Rosemary Basson, a University of British Columbia researcher, found when she interviewed several hundred women.

The conventional wisdom is that desire *precedes* sexual arousal. This works for most men. Men are often coiled springs of desire and easily aroused. Men often describe their libido as a drive similar to hunger or thirst. Twentieth-century sexologists assumed that women's libido was, if not identical, then similar—and that if women didn't feel desire, then something was wrong. . . .

Contrary to the conventional model, for many women, desire is not the cause of lovemaking, but rather, its result. "Women," Basson explains, "often begin sexual experiences feeling sexually neutral." But as things heat up, so do they, and they eventually experience desire.[2]

A healthy responsive libido, in a healthy relationship, means that you're open to sex and have confidence that once you start kissing, touching, and spending time together that desire can build. Now, the crux of responsive libido is that *you actually do respond*. There's a major difference between not having an active desire for sex right now, but knowing you'll have fun when you jump in, and having an active desire *not* to have sex right now. The latter is not a responsive libido—that's simply not wanting sex. If you're in that position frequently, and you never enjoy or desire sex, something deeper may need to be addressed, either with a licensed counselor or a physician, before libido differences are discussed.

Most women do have responsive libidos. Some men have responsive libidos. There is nothing wrong with being responsive. I'd hope we're all a little responsive! Our emotions and our relationship *should* play into our sex drive. If God made us so that we were all 100 percent naturally spontaneous, there would be no need for communication or working on the relationship. We could get by on the fumes of orgasmic sex, and the relationship itself could stay shallow. But because of the way libido works, our drives for connection and for sex end up fueling our relationship and making us closer.

Sex has a sequence that works a bit like a circle:

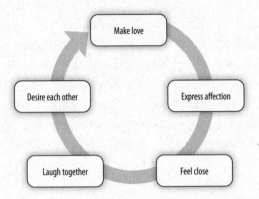

That sequence fuels your marriage. You feel close, you express affection, you have passionate sex and feel connected.

It's tempting to look at that sequence and say, "Exactly! If he would start expressing affection, we could get somewhere." Or, perhaps, "If he would start having sex more, we'd feel closer." But the thing about a circular cycle is that you can jump in anywhere and get the ball rolling. The key question to ask yourself is: Where do *I* need to jump in?

To give that question more context, in this chapter we're looking at normal libido differences, not marriages where someone has

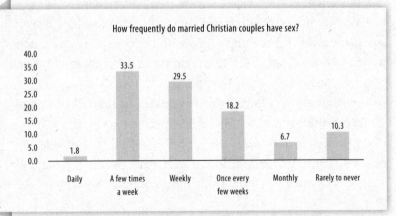

no libido or very little libido (we looked at that in the last two chapters). Before anything else, let's figure out what "normal" is.

Around 65 percent of couples make love at least once a week, with about 17 percent of couples making love very rarely. How much does frequency matter? Well, it turns out that sexual frequency alone does not determine overall marital satisfaction. As I explained in *The Great Sex Rescue*,

> Research has found that frequency is not an accurate predictor [of marital satisfaction]. . . . Sexual satisfaction and interpersonal dynamics are far superior measures, as our survey also revealed. We found that how often a couple has sex is not directly related to their marital quality. However, women who are more sexually satisfied (who consistently orgasm and feel close during sex) reliably have better marriages. How happy your marriage is reflects the quality of your emotional and sexual relationship far more than it does the frequency of intercourse.[3]

Does that mean frequency doesn't matter at all? No, not exactly. It's just that the relationship isn't as straightforward as we may think. A study from York University in Toronto, led by psychology professor Amy Muise, found that more sex is better—to a certain extent. *Time* magazine reported her findings:

> Muise and her study team found that couples who have a lot of sex tend to experience better wellbeing. "Sex is associated with feeling more satisfied in a relationship," Muise says. But beyond once a week, the wellbeing benefits of sex seem to level off. That's not to say that having sex a few times a week (or more) is a bad thing. It just doesn't seem to make couples any happier, she says.[4]

So frequent sex is good, and research defines healthy frequency as at least once a week. Some of you may want sex five or six times a week, but if you're having sex once or twice a week, your husband isn't rejecting you or depriving you. That's actually quite a normal, healthy amount of sex. Others of you may prefer to have sex only every two months or so—and it may be time to prioritize sex more. Let's start with those who may need to dial the libido meter down.

When You're the One with the Spontaneous Libido

A word first to the women with more of a spontaneous libido, married to men who are very responsive: of all the libido scenarios, you likely have the hardest road. Not only are you frustrated and feeling rejected; you've also been told your whole life that your husband's drive is supposed to be insatiable. Reality has kicked you harder than it has most others. We've already covered low libidos for health reasons (or pornography reasons). But what if there's nothing nefarious going on with him, and he simply wants sex less than you do? As one woman told me, "I know he loves me and is attracted to me, but he's totally okay with sex once a week. No need for more. All I want is for him to want me . . . more than once a week. And preferably before I've become so frustrated and am feeling unwanted. And darn it, on my timeline!"

There's nothing wrong with a healthy libido, but if you're constantly resentful, on edge, and moody in a marriage with fairly regular sex, you may have to nurture the discipline of self-control. Often when we feel distant in marriage, those with spontaneous libidos feel their sex drives kick in to soothe any feelings of loneliness or inadequacy. Next time you feel antsy, try a different kind of bid for connection. Sex embodies our spiritual, emotional, and relational selves. If your husband has a low sex drive that isn't due to health problems or addictions, you're still having sex with relative frequency, but you feel distant because you'd like more sex, then the best solution is often to work on your friendship. Jumpstart the sex sequence at the "laugh" stage! Spend more time together. Take a walk after dinner. Find a hobby you can enjoy together.

What if you're a sports or video game widow? Or perhaps you're still engaged and you wonder why your fiancé often finds the latest video game more attractive than spending the afternoon on a walk with you. Many females feel as if they're competing with electronics—and usually losing.

What do you do to recapture him? Standing naked in front of the TV doesn't work; many of my Facebook followers have reported with frustration that their husbands choose baseball over breasts. What's a girl to do?

Many couples live separate lives because they slowly drift apart. One night he comes home, and he's tired so he slumps in front of the screen instead of talking to her. She heads to the computer to scroll Facebook. And soon these separate lives become the norm. When kids arrive, it only gets worse. If you want to spice things up, don't look at the bedroom. Look at the gym. Or the ice rink. Or the restaurant. Do stuff together. Eat dinner at an actual table where you can talk. Often these activities help you feel connected, and then, even if sex doesn't always follow, at least you feel kindlier toward each other.

When His Responsive Libido Just Doesn't Respond

But sometimes it's not only that your husband has a lower libido than you; it's that he genuinely has an abnormally low libido, hardly ever initiating sex and rarely responding when you do. In a given population, it's only natural that some men will fall on either end of the libido spectrum—some desire sex more than usual, and some less. Your husband's sex drive may be atypical, but that doesn't mean it's pathologically atypical. Or, to put it in layman's terms, it may not be normal, but that doesn't mean there's necessarily sin or medical issues at play (although, of course, this should be verified).

That's hardly a comfort, though, when you're lying in bed

wanting to make love and he's already snoring. Listen to this twenty-nine-year-old woman, married for four years, explain how frustrated she is:

> The thing that we've fought about the most in our marriage is our sex life. I feel like I've fallen into some strange parallel universe where I have to beg my husband to have sex with me! I'm attractive, keep myself looking nice, and I'm not overweight . . . and I've tried everything. In most marriage books, I can usually relate more to the sections about frustrated husbands wanting more sex from their wives. The only problem is, there's no advice for me to turn to! Either everyone assumes that he's using pornography (he's not) or that he's cheating (he's definitely not), or that I'm doing something wrong as a wife, and trust me, I've tried everything.
>
> It's been difficult for us, and I've started to hate approaching him for sex, because I know that I have a high likelihood of being turned down. Everything else in our relationship is great—our friendship, our compatibility, our love for each other—but we just don't "click" when it comes to how often we each need sex. He's like a sex camel—he could go for weeks. I need it/want it about three to four times a week.
>
> All the books make me feel like some sort of sex addict or like I'm not really a feminine woman because I want sex and I have actual physical desire for it—not just for the hand holding and to be made to feel loved, but because women, like men, sometimes need sex. I just don't know what to do anymore, and I feel helpless about the future of our sexual relationship.

Are you married to a sex camel too? Talk to your husband about how you feel. Assuming you've already dealt with any possible medical problems as we talked about in the last chapter, and you've ruled out pornography use or other hidden sexual sins, now may be the time to visit a licensed counselor because infrequent sex isn't healthy in your marriage and should be addressed. It could be that nothing will give you the frequency of sex you most desire. By focusing on your friendship and building connection in other ways despite sexual frustration, you will still lower the stress in your marriage while you work through this issue. That has dual benefits: his libido will likely grow, and your ability to handle the dry spells will likely grow too.

How Does That Sequence Work for Responsive-Desire People?

Maybe you're the more sexually responsive one, and desire doesn't register easily. Now, if you're in the group of women who enjoy a healthy frequency of sex, and your husband would prefer every day or multiple times a day, he may need to learn some contentment and self-control.

But many women want sex far less often than what research has found is the healthy amount for a relationship. You may want me to say, "If he wants it a lot, that's his problem," and to a certain extent, that may be true. Our survey of twenty thousand women found that women who stop having sex are far more likely to feel emotionally distant from their husbands during sex, to be married to porn users, to be in marriages with sexual dysfunction, to have low marital satisfaction, and to struggle with orgasm. If any of those apply to you, *fix those issues first*. Also know that in the companion book to this one, *The Good Guy's Guide to Great Sex*, there is a whole chapter telling guys how they need to consider your needs and figure out how to unlock your libido rather than pressuring you or guilting you into sex.

But provided those five factors do not apply to you, let's look at how that sex sequence can fuel a marriage.

A few years ago I was scheduled to be away speaking for a few days, and the night before I left, I was rather distracted. So we didn't *you know*. I arrived home from that trip at midnight, so we didn't *you know*. The next night I knew he was hoping for it, and normally it would have happened. I like sex too, after all. But I was tired and grumpy. So we didn't. And neither of us slept well.

The night after that I threw myself into it, we had a great time, and all was well. The next day Keith bought me flowers. *Sex flowers.*

And I thought, "Why do I get flowers on the days after we make love and not after the days we don't?" I grew angry. But after I came back to earth and thought about that sequence, I figured out what the issue was. Keith was simply expressing affection because we had just made love!

I mistakenly read all sorts of perverse motives into his flower purchase, assuming his thoughts ran something like this: *She made love to me, so she needs to be rewarded. I need to withhold romance and affection when she doesn't perform and give it to her only when she does so she starts acting the way I want her to.* That's not what he was thinking at all.

Here's the truth: women have surges of a hormone called oxytocin more frequently than men do. It's the bonding hormone. It's present when we make love, when we nurse our babies, when we hug our kids. Men experience their biggest surge of oxytocin when they make love, which is why they feel close to us afterward and are often so lovey-dovey the next day. It's not to be manipulative; it's because they honestly feel attached and affectionate (and if he is being manipulative, that's not a sex problem but a relationship one; please see a licensed counselor).

> Better sex builds companionship.

That's why we need to see friendship and sex as a sequence. Yes, companionship builds better sex. But also, *better sex builds companionship.*

Often we lower-drive women discount sex and put more

emphasis on friendship. We feel that sex is a baser need, while friendship is superior. In doing so, we forget the missing ingredient: men are more likely to feel lovey-dovey toward us when they also feel sexually connected to us.

Having sex just for the sake of having sex can degrade it. But *in an already healthy marriage*, frequent sex has benefits that spill into the rest of your relationship.

Maintaining regular sex boosts your friendship. In the friendship-sex sequence, one thing leads to the other, and as each improves, you grow closer and closer. And that has repercussions on other aspects of your life too!

What is the effect of a wife having frequent, satisfying sex on a couple's marital and sexual satisfaction? (How many times more or less likely are they to experience the following?)	
I feel that my husband considers my needs, desires, and wants in our marriage as much as he does his own	5.3
I am satisfied with the amount of housework my husband does	2.6
I am confident my husband is not tempted by other women	2.7
When we have conflict, I don't feel like my husband really hears me	-3.2
I often feel uncomfortable about how my husband looks at other women when we are in public	-3.8

I'm Not Talking about Obligation Sex

We've talked about prioritizing sex more, or choosing to have sex even if you'd rather binge watch season thirteen of your favorite show, knowing that if you do, you'll feel great afterward. But that's not the same as having sex out of obligation. No one is required to give their husband sex when he wants it, and his desire for sex is not more important than your desire for sleep or for time to yourself to rejuvenate. Our study found that when women believe they're *obligated* to have sex when their husbands want it, a lot of bad things happen, including higher rates of vaginismus and lower rates of arousal.[5]

Kay loved sex before she had children, but her third labor brought not only a new baby but also a bad tear and postpartum depression. The next few months were like a fog. Once she was physically healed, she went back to initiating sex every seventy-two hours, like clockwork, because she had been told in Christian circles how much her husband needed it and how she shouldn't deprive him. But her libido never bounced back. While she used to be orgasmic, her body no longer responded.

After a few years, she sat her husband down and told him she couldn't keep going like this. He was flabbergasted; he hadn't known she initiated out of guilt. He assured her that he never wanted her to do anything she didn't want to do, and from now on, even if they were in the middle of intercourse and she wanted to stop, he wanted her to tell him. Kay began speaking up, and in doing so, she felt her sexuality return. Duty had killed it, but knowing that her husband gave her the freedom to say no awakened her desire to say yes. And so they've settled into a new routine where they have sex . . . *every seventy-two hours*! But this time it's because she wants to, not because she feels like she has to.

Many of us have grown up hearing messages in evangelical church culture that tell us to have sex under threat—so he won't have an affair, lust, or watch porn. Believing these kinds of messages artificially lowers a woman's libido. If you're hanging on to obligation messages or threatening messages, talk to your husband. Talk to a licensed counselor, or read my book *The Great Sex Rescue*. Maybe all you need to want to say yes is to realize God doesn't get mad if you say no.

With that as the context, please understand that everything I'm saying in this chapter is not to guilt you into something or make you feel like sex is an obligation. I want you to understand that you are a sexual being, that sex is something worth prioritizing, that this is a way to show love to your husband, and most of all that sex is something amazing you do not want to miss out on!

There's also a reason that this chapter is at the end of the book. The importance of prioritizing sex is the message to hear *after* you've figured out the orgasm piece, *after* you've dealt with any porn issues, and *after* you've received counseling for sexual trauma or dealt with the ghosts in your past. Once sex is physically great, and once your relationship is built on trust, intimacy, and safety, *then* make sure you prioritize sex and enjoy all the passion God meant for both of you.

How Rejection Can Affect Your Husband

The issue that frequently lands men on my blog is feeling sexually rejected by their wives. Listen to these men:

- "I don't feel loved because my wife doesn't want sex. I feel like she doesn't want me personally."
- "You know there is a lack of interest, but you don't really know why. You start to think, What is wrong with me?"
- "I feel rejected, like my wants, needs, and desires don't matter."
- "It really hurts. I feel like a failure and a horrible husband because she almost never lets us have sex. It doesn't make sense, but it's how I feel."

Speaking as one who has done my share of rejecting, I found these responses rather humbling. Looking back, I could always see the many good reasons I had for saying no to sex, and if he was hurt, I thought Keith was exaggerating. But listening to focus groups and our survey results, when I wasn't emotionally involved in the situation, I began to sympathize. Lack of sex hurts not only sexual satisfaction but marital satisfaction too, including our own.

Often we can't hear our husband's pain because we're so wrapped up in what we're feeling. We're tired and don't want to be bothered. We feel that they want only one thing and don't value us.

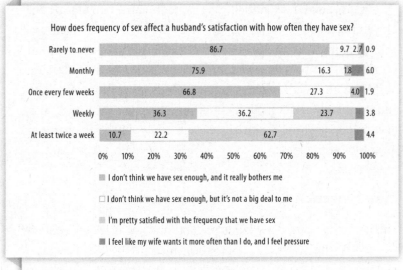

How does frequency of sex affect a husband's satisfaction with how often they have sex?

Rarely to never	86.7	9.7	2.7	0.9
Monthly	75.9	16.3	1.8	6.0
Once every few weeks	66.8	27.3	4.0	1.9
Weekly	36.3	36.2	23.7	3.8
At least twice a week	10.7 / 22.2	62.7		4.4

0% 10% 20% 30% 40% 50% 60% 70% 80% 90% 100%

■ I don't think we have sex enough, and it really bothers me

☐ I don't think we have sex enough, but it's not a big deal to me

▨ I'm pretty satisfied with the frequency that we have sex

■ I feel like my wife wants it more often than I do, and I feel pressure

We feel under pressure to perform. In our early years of marriage, Keith and I fought frequently about my lack of desire, even after my vaginismus had cleared up. He would say, "I just want you to want me!" and I would protest, "But I do want you! I want you as my husband! I want you to be happy! I want you with me always!"

What he wanted was for me to jump him. And I couldn't do that because somehow it felt like lying. I didn't particularly want to make love. Sure, I'd do it if he started it, but it wasn't like I was sitting there, engines ready to go, waiting to take off. I would much rather watch a movie, read a book, cuddle, or just about anything. And I was so, so tired of him wanting it all the time. More than that, I was tired of him not accepting me. He wanted me to want to make love as much as he did—and how could I force myself to do that?

Over the years, God helped me to see my husband's point of view. Sex is vulnerable and intimate and is often a way we check in on the relationship. If we're constantly rejected in favor of Netflix or scrolling through Instagram, that can be devastating. And when the lower-drive spouse scoffs at those feelings of rejection, that's telling the higher-drive spouse you think their feelings are invalid.

Here's what a forty-year-old woman, married ten years, said:

I have a really low sex drive due to medical issues (medication has helped, but not as much as we'd like). I probably want to about once a week. He wants to every day, multiple times! He says I'm just so dang sexy. LOL. But he does get frustrated if I never want to or he feels like I'm "giving in." We've talked about it a lot and tried different things, and I've found that if I say yes willingly if there's not a good reason for me to say no (feel bad, bad timing), and we take plenty of time for foreplay, my sex drive does catch up eventually and I can enjoy myself fully. That makes him feel like the king of the world, and now he can accept that I have a good reason to say no when I do. Our sex life has never been better! But it has taken us time to get to this point—if we weren't so committed to this relationship, I think it would have been a major issue.

She decided that if she didn't have a good reason for saying no, she would say yes. And she found that her sex drive often caught up because he did his part in working with her sexual response too. I love how he feels like he's "king of the world"—and also that the couple has learned how not just to say "yes" more frequently, but that he has also learned to have a healthy relationship with "no."

Here's how another woman came to her epiphany of what she was doing to her husband:

About five years ago, my husband was so frustrated with being turned down so many times that he told me that from now on it was up to me to decide when we would make love. He wrote a long letter that showed me that he felt neglected by me giving all my attention and energy to our three kids. He felt he only got leftovers. We had removed the word divorce from our dictionary years ago, and he reaffirmed his commitment to me as a person, his wife, and mate and to being a super involved dad—but just couldn't live with the lack of sexual connection and activity. He told me (in the letter) that he would always be ready if and when I was in the mood. That was one of the most tearful nights we've spent as I read his letter (sitting next to him), and we just held each other for the rest of the night.

In those next four years, he rarely initiated and just waited on me. God mightily changed my heart and my attitude. I began to take more initiative and got more interested in him and spending time with him (his primary love language). Our sex life has changed profoundly. We are much more playful, and while we still have a few differences, it is so much better now.

In the last year or so, he has begun to initiate some too, and our sex life is beginning to be more mutual. God is so good!

In a way, I'm sad we waited so long to get this right.

This forty-eight-year-old woman, married for over a quarter of a century, didn't figure things out until well into the third decade of her marriage. Today they make love three or four times a week, and she rates every part of her relationship as "really great." They have close spiritual and emotional connection; he shares the load around the house; they communicate well. Sex didn't only exist in the physical part of her relationship; it impacted everything else too. They feel much closer now. But take heed of her last sentence: "I'm sad we waited so long to get this right."

Reclaim Your Own Sex Drive

I think many women believe that *he wants it all the time, and I will never be enough for him, so there's no point in trying.* Yet in general that's not true (and if your husband insists on weird sex or sex multiple times a day, then please see a licensed counselor).[6]

At one point when I was recovering from my sexual problems in the first few years of our marriage, I made a commitment to make love to Keith whenever he asked. I was so proud of myself. I was a great wife. I was selfless. I was amazing! Surreptitiously I grabbed a pocket calendar and proudly started circling the days we made love.

Then, after several weeks of what I thought was fairly frequent sex, my husband turned to me and moaned, "I feel like we never make love." I whipped out that calendar and told him, "You have nothing to complain about, buddy." That led to a rather interesting—and heated—discussion. But finally I understood something. Men don't want to be placated. They want to be wanted.

A good husband doesn't want his wife to "let" him make love to her; he wants her to engage in the process. That means emotionally deciding to jump in—deciding to enjoy it. Most men want to make her toes curl. It isn't only about whether *he* experiences pleasure; it's whether he can give *you* pleasure (assuming, of course, he's taken the time to learn how your body responds). It's hard for a husband to believe that you're proud of him and that you're happy to be married to him if you don't also want him sexually. And the best way to show your husband you want him is by initiating sex every now and then.

> Men don't want to be placated. They want to be wanted.

Initiation Is the Key to Many a Husband's Heart

Initiating sex may be the last thing you want to do for a host of reasons. You may be exhausted. You may feel distant. You may wonder if it will really be relaxing for you.

If you start initiating, a lot of those issues may diminish in importance. If you initiate, you can set the tone and the direction. Perhaps lately he has been rushing sex and you haven't enjoyed it as much as you'd like. If you initiate, you can make sure the angle and pressure are right. You can slow things down. So why not jump in with the express purpose of showing him anew how much you enjoy sex when you both deliberately pursue your pleasure?

One young wife, who has been married for two years, finds that initiating helps her in other ways too. She says, "I have this weird issue about being touched sometimes, and I know that my husband has a stronger sex drive than I do. I tend to initiate so that I am the one in control—doing the touching and being able to determine when we have sex."

When you have sexual issues, sometimes initiating can help you feel more comfortable and you're more able to enjoy yourself.

What about other problems? Let's say you feel as if he is distant. There's nothing particularly wrong with the marriage, but you often pick at each other. Initiating sex can bring down that tension by conveying to him, "I enjoy having fun with you." Then you get that sex sequence going in a positive direction! So if you feel like you're in a bit of a rut, why not take that first step toward repairing the rift?

Jump In!

Part of our problem with initiating is that we have misconceptions of what sex is supposed to look like. We marry with expectations that sex will be a glorious, rip-roaring fun, awesome experience. If night comes and we aren't ravenously panting, waiting for that glorious, rip-roaring fun, awesome experience, we women feel we should wait until we're "in the mood."

To make love when you don't feel like it seems somehow like lying. But remember that difference between wanting *not* to have sex and simply having a responsive libido. Again, I'm not advocating making love no matter what—even if he's having an affair, he's into pornography, or he makes you feel dirty. But if he simply has a higher libido and you don't consider his perspective, your own libido becomes the sole determining factor in whether you make love. You hold all the cards; your husband holds none.

We responsive-libido women need to take some initiative. We need to say occasionally—not every night, but consistently and regularly—"I want you." And if we get our minds in gear, our bodies will follow. We may not feel in the mood beforehand, but we can get in the mood if we decide to because sex is mostly in our heads. Claim the power of that responsive libido! Instead of waiting for your body to magically tell you, "I want to get it on!" you can give your body a rah-rah lecture. *I've had a long day and people have been wanting things from me since I got up this morning. I deserve to feel amazing, and I want to end this day in my husband's arms. So we are going to do this—and it's going to be awesome!*

When our girls were young, we'd often take them to a hotel as a treat so we could all enjoy the pool. Keith and the girls would jump in and splash and play Marco Polo, and I would shiver on the top step, slowly dipping my toe down to the second step, all the while saying to myself, "It's so cold!" Little by little, I'd submerge myself more, tottering on my tiptoes so I didn't have to get wetter than necessary. And finally, after twenty minutes of wobbling, I'd count to three about seventeen times before diving in.

By that time the kids were ready to get out.

I didn't save myself from feeling cold; I was freezing anyway. I would have had a much better time if I had just dived in to begin with.

It's the same with sex. Many times we women lie in bed wondering if we want to have sex. The conversation in our heads goes something like this: *Do I want to tonight?* I don't know. *Does he?* Probably. *Is he lying there waiting for me to make the first move? Or is he already asleep?* Nope, it doesn't sound like he's sleeping. He's probably thinking about sex. *Should I do something?* I'm not sure. It's 11:15 now, and I have to be up by 6:45. *Will I be too tired in the morning if we make love? How long will it take?*

The silly thing is that if you had jumped him in the beginning, you could be asleep by now, satisfied and relaxed. Instead of torturing yourself for half an hour trying to decide if you might be in the mood, decide that it's going to be amazing, and see what happens! And, hey, then you'll sleep better too.

Libido is largely a "use it or lose it" phenomenon. Those who have sex frequently are far more likely to think about sex and to become aroused faster than those who don't have sex often. That's what this twenty-seven-year-old found:

> I feel that his drive is abnormally high and mine is abnormally low. (He agrees mine is low but thinks his is normal—what he would compare it to, I don't know!) He would like to be having sex daily; I'd be content with once a week. . . . We've settled into three-ish times per week usually, though that varies. I have learned through experience that if I just do it more—even if I'm not in the mood, if I will make the time—then I end up enjoying it, and it increases my own desire. So I have made efforts over the last couple of years to simply do it more often, and it has definitely helped my drive.

Don't be like "hotel pool" Sheila, hovering on the first step of the swimming pool, missing out on all the fun. You don't need to be panting before you make love; that will come if your brain is in gear. Trust that if you jump in, your body will follow!

CHAPTER 11

Hungering for Each Other

One summer when our daughters were younger, we sent them off to summer camp while my husband and I escaped to the Couples Resort, a posh getaway near Algonquin Provincial Park in southeastern Ontario. Everything about that resort shouted "sex," from the logo of a couple intertwined to the king-size beds and Jacuzzis.

The first day we played a lot of tennis and did a few other physical activities to work up an appetite. We had heard that the food at this place was amazing, so I was salivating as they seated us for dinner.

To begin the evening, the waiter presented us with the tiniest little nibble to "whet your appetite." It was tasty and interesting, but it was only about a bite big. When the appetizers arrived, we found they were rather size-challenged too. Just enough was presented to seduce our taste buds.

While the appetizers were delectable, I became mildly teed off. How about a huge Caesar salad or a thick clam chowder? Sure, the food was scrumptious, but it was hardly enough to fill up a squirrel. And I was hungry.

But then it occurred to me that this resort was trying to make an *experience* out of eating. They weren't trying to fill us up; they were trying to tease us for what would come next. And because there was a lag of about twenty minutes between courses, by the time the next course came, we were ready for it!

Truck Stop versus Resort

Too often we see sex like a truck stop diner instead of like that gourmet resort. Sex becomes utilitarian; we have it because we need to. Men are "hungry," so they need to "eat," so let's satisfy that craving so we can move on with the rest of our lives.

If that's our attitude, we're diminishing sex. Making love is not only about releasing physical urges, although it is about that. It's also the means to building deep, intimate connections in our relationship, and so it should be savored.

For women, savoring something is hard when we view it from that utilitarian angle. Maybe you don't "hunger" for sex the way your husband does. If we think of sex as something just to satisfy a hunger, then it's all too easy to put it on the back burner. And what if your husband is hungry but you're not? Then sex becomes "just for him," and you feel used.

That's why we need to get out of the diner mentality and get into the five-star restaurant mentality. Sex should be something that *awakens* hunger, not only something that satiates it. God created sex to be an integral part of our marriages, not only to satisfy a need but also to celebrate and reaffirm our unions. When we eat simply so we aren't hungry anymore, the purpose is to make the hunger go away so we can get on with our "real" lives. But a sexual relationship that is

> Sex should be something that *awakens* hunger, not only something that satiates it.

a deeply intimate, emotionally close, and mutually satisfying "five-star" experience can *be* our real lives if we work to make it happen.

Let's not lose touch with reality, though. I'm not arguing that every time you make love it has to be some mind-blowing experience where the earth moves. Life isn't like that. Each individual encounter may not be earth-shattering, but the sum total of the relationship should reflect that deep, intimate experience. And let me suggest that when we make love in the context of a Christian marriage, with God at the center, our relationship *should* reflect that. What makes it stupendous isn't only our feelings during each sexual episode but also the fact that we are joining more than just our physical bodies—we are joining our very selves. That joining is blessed and a blessing.

So sometimes you'll make love simply because you're anxious, on edge, or tired, and you need something to help you calm down. Sometimes you'll make love because you want to give him a gift even though you're pretty zonked yourself. Sometimes you'll have a quickie because the kids will be up in a minute and you're racing the clock. And sometimes you may even make love because you're incredibly aroused from thinking of something hot that you and your husband did earlier.

None of that is wrong. In fact, it's all pretty great! But sex, in the big picture, is about expressing deep connection, and while each individual encounter doesn't have to feel profound, some of them should. We should be moving toward marriage relationships in which we can act out of a deep hunger. So how do we do that?

Whetting Your Appetite

The Couples Resort took something that could have been just physical satisfaction—food—and turned it into something to be savored. I think married couples could learn a lot about how to enhance our sex lives simply by studying how five-star restaurants make eating a luscious experience.

Food, like sex, is a physical hunger, but it doesn't have to be *just* a physical hunger or even primarily a physical hunger. It can be used to build relationships and forge intimacy. Sure, you could eat at a McDonald's drive through or a truck stop, but if you had the choice, wouldn't you rather have steak and potatoes with all the fixings? If we took a similar perspective on our sex lives—that it is a hunger meant to be stirred, an experience to be enjoyed, not just a need to be quenched—we'd experience and enjoy that spiritual connection much more. So let's see how some rituals that make eating more meaningful can also make sex more meaningful.

The Dedication

Before eating at a fancy event, after the food arrives, traditionally guests have a dedication, in either the form of a prayer or a toast or both. We lift our glasses and say something wonderful about our host or the reason for being together.

Who brought you together? God. God made sex, God likes sex, and God celebrates sex—in the right context. And marriage is the right context, so you're good to go! Part of seeing sex in its proper light and getting rid of any shame we may feel about it is inviting God in. This is especially important if you're still getting used to each other's bodies or if you're healing from pornography, abuse, or a breach of trust.

But even if everything's A-OK, praying and reading Scripture together can make sex even hotter. As we remind ourselves of who God is, we frequently feel even closer to each other. If you don't believe me, listen to this:

> Like an apple tree among the trees of the forest
>> is my beloved among the young men.
> I delight to sit in his shade,
>> and his fruit is sweet to my taste.
> Let him lead me to the banquet hall,
>> and let his banner over me be love.

> Strengthen me with raisins,
> > refresh me with apples,
> > for I am faint with love.

—Song of Songs 2:3–5

Or how about this:

> Come, all you who are thirsty,
> > come to the waters;
> and you who have no money,
> > come, buy and eat!
> Come, buy wine and milk
> > without money and without cost.
> Why spend money on what is not bread,
> > and your labor on what does not satisfy?
> Listen, listen to me, and eat what is good,
> > and you will delight in the richest of fare.

—Isaiah 55:1–2

Those are both Scripture passages—beautiful, vivid ones about appetites. Appetites for God and for one's spouse. And the Bible has many more such passages. When we feel closest to God, we also tend to feel drawn to our mates, and so one of the best ways you can make sex far more meaningful and exciting is to draw together spiritually *first*. If you're not used to doing devotions or praying together, it doesn't have to be a big production. Read a psalm together. Pray together while you're lying entwined in each other's arms. Bring God in, and you'll find your physical intimacy far more meaningful.

The Setting

When my husband and I venture out for an anniversary dinner, we always head to a place with candles. There's something about eating by candlelight that seems romantic, even if it's only that we don't notice our own imperfections. Food somehow tastes better on a lovely tablecloth, with the right music for ambience, and with candlelight flickering in your beloved's eyes.

The setting matters for sex too. Have you ever seen a movie where the breathless couple collapses into a bed of hay in a barn to make love? It's supposed to be all romantic, but when I watch that, all I can think is, "Wouldn't that be scratchy?" I have similar issues with the "making love in a field" scenes. What about ants crawling where you really don't want them?

Part of having fun together and feeling close is having a nice *place* to have fun, where you can relax, share, and talk, as well as roll around in the sheets. So ensure that your bedroom is a place where fun of all sorts can happen—and where you'll want it to happen.

Some bedrooms become a repository for all our junk. We don't know where else to put it, so it ends up piled in a corner by the bed. And since that bed is so deliciously large, with a nice big surface at a good height, why not sort laundry on it? Of course, chances are you won't get everything folded during the day, and you'll forget all about it until the evening, when you have to throw the laundry onto the floor anyway to climb into bed, but it's worth a try.

Let's be frank, girls: your bedroom should be the most important room in the house—more important than the kitchen, the living room, or the family room. The family functions well when the couple functions well. You will be a better parent if you and your husband feel intimate. And you won't feel intimate in a bedroom that's a mess. So don't use your bedroom as a storage room!

And that means keeping your work out of the bedroom too. Don't leave files from work around the bedroom, and banish electronic distractions. Keep it as a place for relaxation so that when you're in the bedroom, you're together talking, not watching *CSI* before bed. When my husband and I watch a movie at night, we do it in the family room. Then we have to get up, turn off the lights, and retire to the bedroom. We're both awake. We're both climbing into bed at the same time. And then we can talk, snuggle, or whatever!

Your bedroom is for your relationship. Make sure it's conducive to that. Candles help. Comfortable pillows and a nice mattress help. A bed that doesn't squeak is rather important, especially as children age. I know furniture and bedding can be expensive, but don't scrimp on this area of the house. Make your bedroom a romantic oasis where you can escape into each other's arms, not somewhere all the stuff in the house gets dumped, making you feel guilty every time you see it. This is a place to reserve for you and your husband and the sexual side of your relationship.

The Presentation

Have you ever had one of those molten lava cakes for dessert at a posh restaurant? You can buy them in the freezer section of the grocery store and then pop them into the microwave, and they're still yummy with soft, runny chocolate in the middle, with spongy cake on the outside. But in a restaurant they're even better because they come drizzled with cream and raspberry sauce and sprinkled with icing sugar, artistically arranged in the middle of an oversized plate, with a sprig of mint and a hint of cocoa. The restaurant takes that same grocery store molten lava cake and turns it into a scrumptious work of art by presenting it delectably.

Presentation with food matters, and it matters with sex too. Yet how many of us tend to look frumpy for the hubby? Often the only time we put effort into looking good is when we're heading out somewhere—to work, church, or even shopping. We take care to look attractive for strangers but not for our husbands.

When I speak to women, I use a nightgown for a prop. It's oversized, it's flannel, and it leaves everything to the imagination. They say a little mystery is a good thing; that may be true, but a lot is too much. When I hold it up, everyone laughs because they can relate to this hideous monstrosity. Of course, some people wear flannel like this because their husbands insist on keeping the house at fifty degrees at night. To those men, I like to say, "If you want to turn up the heat in the bedroom, you might actually want to *turn up the heat*." But what do you wear to bed? Do you take care to wear something attractive, or something that looks like you're not even trying?

And what about our husbands? Several years ago our family started a new tradition of buying matching pajamas every Christmas so we can take those corny Christmas photos. But I quickly realized that one of the wonderful side benefits is that my husband now has sleek looking pj's, rather than coming to bed in scrubs and old painting T-shirts. While I love that he's a doctor, when we're trying to get hot and heavy, I don't want to think about him resuscitating babies. When I realized how much I loved his new pajamas, I bought him better underwear too. Now I love catching a peek before he gets dressed in the morning!

Presentation isn't just about clothes or makeup, though. My hometown has two seasons: winter and construction. And winter is substantially longer. We all celebrate when the warm weather arrives, and we shove the hats, mittens, scarves, and winter coats away and replace them with T-shirts, flip-flops, and happiness.

And razors.

After all, when it's cold out, what's the point of shaving? No one's going to see our legs or our armpits until bathing suit season comes around, so many of us northern girls let ourselves go in the winter. That's a little rough on our husbands, in more ways than one.

Recently I was discussing grooming on my blog, and after several women made the point that God values the inside not the outside, and so we should never worry about appearance, one commenter vigorously disagreed.

I have never understood the "letting myself go" [mentality]. Looking frazzled and unkempt on the outside does not make your heart godlier on the inside. . . .

My husband loves it when I dress it up for him, so I do that almost every day . . . and it is not even all about makeup—which I only wear sparingly; it's about taking care of myself so I feel sexy. And when I feel sexy, I am able to come across as sexy.

Sex is not only about the body but is also done with the body, and so presenting our bodies well is a way to serve each other. So before your husband gets home tonight—or before you get home tonight—take an extra minute to apply some lipstick (if that's your thing), brush your hair, and put on some earrings (if you don't have babies who will pull them!). Make that effort to look great for him—not because you're trying to compete with a supermodel, or because you're trying to compete with pornography, or because you're buying into our culture's take on beauty, but simply because you love him and want to show off for him. You want to seduce him. You want to be beautiful for him. You even want to turn him on! What guy wouldn't like that?

But what if it's your husband who could use a razor? Or even a toothbrush a little more often? Speak up! Many women write in to my blog wondering what to do about husbands who keep asking for sex but fail to realize that stinky and sexy don't go together. Make showering and brushing your teeth part of foreplay. And if he comes to bed without brushing his teeth, ask him to fix it. "Brush your teeth first, please, honey!" Pretending nothing's wrong and then scooching to the far side of the bed is going to hurt your marriage in the long run far more than a few awkward conversations about better hygiene.

The Appetizer

In a diner, the purpose of the appetizer is to start filling you up. In a five-star restaurant, the purpose is to prepare your mouth for the tastes to come. We need sexual appetizers too—little things that start our own minds and bodies going in the right direction.

Those of us who waited to make love until we were married spent a significant amount of time flirting. We whispered, "I can't wait until we can . . . " We giggled at double entendres. We had breathless make-out sessions. But then we married, and for many of us that flirting came to a standstill. Part of the reason is that we no longer eagerly anticipated sex, but another significant factor is that we women can be reticent about putting a down payment on something we may not want to buy later.

That's why kissing disappears from many new marriage relationships. We stop kissing our mates because they often interpret it as a promise of what's to come. We figure the best way to make sure we don't promise something we won't deliver on is simply not to promise in the first place. One woman admitted, "I'm afraid to do too much touching because I'm afraid it will lead to sex. I don't get much satisfaction from sex, so I try to avoid physical affection."

Don't fall into this trap! Most women need a catalyst for sexual interest, whether it be physical or mental. Flirting and kissing are part of that process. If we give up on expressions of intimacy because we're afraid we may not want to deliver later, it's almost guaranteed that we *won't* want to deliver later, because we've removed our own tools to get us there!

One of the strangest mental flips you may have to make as a wife is that once you're married, sex is no longer something to run from. Here's how one woman described this change in mindset:

> I wish that in the months leading up to my wedding I'd had some help in making the psychological switch from "chaste virgin" to "sexual wife." I engaged in the act of sex from my wedding night onward, but I did not make the mental switch. I was uncomfortable with my own sexuality for years. I have been married seven years this month, and it has been just the

last three to four months that I have realized this about myself and finally made the change. It has made my sex life blossom so much, and I wish I had done it years ago.

Even if you were sexually active before marriage, you could still find this mentality difficult. No matter what our backgrounds before we were married, we need to think of the wedding as a clean break, the birth of a new person—because that's what it is. No longer are you only you; you and your husband have become one, and that means you can view the physical side of your relationship in a whole new way.

It's okay to think about sex during the day! You can even let him in on it. Send him sexy texts to tell him what's going through your mind (the act of sending them may be what gets you thinking about it in the first place). Make them X-rated if you so wish and you're sure nobody will see his phone! But if you're shy or worried about privacy, even texting "still tingling from last night," "I can't wait for you to get home," or "I have something in store for you" will remind both of you how much fun you can have together.

> Flirt with the expectation that you *will* want to tonight—or at least very soon.

If you flirt throughout the day and kiss your husband passionately when you're together, it's not only him who starts thinking about plans for the evening—you do too! Now don't do this if you're regularly going to say no. Instead, flirt with the expectation that you *will* want to tonight—or at least very soon. Feed your own sexual appetite. It's not just about whetting his but also whetting your own by reminding yourself that you are a sexual being too!

The Spices

Gourmet restaurants know that steak doesn't have to be served with peppercorn sauce. Fish doesn't need tartar sauce. Soup can even be made of fruit, mint can be served with meat, and flowers can be a garnish. The restaurant doesn't have to do the expected.

And that's true for married lovers too. You don't always have to make love at night when you're heading to bed. You don't even always have to make love in the bedroom. You can be creative and mix it up a little.

Finding times that work for sex can be a challenge. With many couples facing shift work scheduling conflicts, how can we relegate our sex lives to that hour between 10:30 p.m. and 11:30 p.m., when most of us head to bed? Even if shift work isn't a factor, many of us turn in at different times, depending on our sleep needs and preferences. So we have to find other times to make love.

For some couples, having sex first thing in the morning is easier than at night because at least they're in bed together. Others use the time when children are napping or sleeping, regardless of the time of day. And when couples are first married and babies aren't on the scene yet, any time of day can work. Don't wait for nightfall to wind up in the bedroom together. And if you're heading up to bed but your husband isn't following, maybe you need to send him a signal that sleep is not what you had planned.

Even with kids in the house, a quickie during the day leaves you laughing afterward. We women may not get that aroused (foreplay's often squeezed out when you're trying to beat the clock or be fast enough that the children won't realize you're not in the kitchen anymore), but he'll wear a smile on his face all day long. And then you can ask him to return the favor later!

When it comes to making love, there are no hard-and-fast rules about the when and the where, as long as you're private. So be creative. You don't always have to serve things at the same time in the same place in the same way.

The Menu

And you don't have to serve the same *thing* all the time either. As wonderful as the food was at that resort, I didn't want the same thing every night. Sometimes I had the salmon. One night I had scallops. Naturally I sampled the steak. Food, no matter how good, gets boring if you eat too much of the same thing.

Be careful of the ruts in your intimate life too. We all hit them—when we're tired, when we make love thinking it's "just for him," when we're preoccupied with something else. It's hard to feel a connection when sex becomes routine. My friend Christie Rayburn, who cohosted the television show *Marriage Uncensored*, once confessed to her audience that she and her husband Mark have a "three in a row—no-no" rule. They don't let themselves have sex three times in a row in the same position. They're always switching it up so they don't hit that rut.

Sometimes we women steer away from more adventure in bed because for us one position tends to work best. If you tend to orgasm best in one position, that's okay. But that doesn't mean you have to spend your whole sexual encounter that way. You can still spice it up. Start in a new position, even if you have to finish in "old faithful" (whatever that may be for you). Start in a different room. Do something different (like spending some time using your mouth or your hands to turn him on). As you try something new, your body may respond unexpectedly. And the confidence you'll gain by seeing the effect on your husband will likely boost your libido as well. So every now and then, challenge yourself to be a little more adventurous. You may find it's an awfully fun game!

The Enjoyment

I'm the better cook in our marriage. I often banish people from the kitchen every night at 4:30 p.m. when I prepare dinner because this is my sacred time. I love sampling new spice blends, transforming leftovers into something gourmet, and eating veggies from our garden.

But one Valentine's Day, Keith wanted to cook for me. He planned a whole menu, including a shrimp appetizer, a steak and asparagus main course, and a chocolate cheesecake dessert. The only problem was that he hadn't figured out how to have everything ready at the same time, so he was constantly getting up from the table to take the veggies off the heat or to check the steak. I ended up eating my dinner mostly alone. He cooked for me, but he didn't sit down to enjoy it himself.

We laugh about that now, but as this book wraps up, one of the big-picture ideas I want you to keep with you is that while it's wonderful to be generous in bed and give to your husband, it's just as important to allow yourself to receive. When you understand that sex was not created just for him, with you as an afterthought, but see it instead as something beautiful that you enjoy together, then it will be not only more fun but more meaningful as well. When you make love not just to give but allow yourself to receive, then you become more vulnerable, more transparent, more naked. You "know" each other on a much deeper level.

Some of us need to be challenged to give more. We need to make sex more of a priority. So let me ask: Wouldn't you love to long for sex? Wouldn't it be fun to live with abandon, at least for a few minutes every few nights? Wouldn't you love to feel bliss, to feel his love, to laugh? Then make it happen!

Some of us also need to be challenged to let ourselves receive. Sex isn't something you rush through to check off your to-do list and feel like an awesome wife; it's something where you allow yourself to be served too—where you open up, let your guard down, and lose all reserve. If you have sexual insecurities, that's okay. I did too. Deal with them. Talk to someone. Don't settle for the status quo. You aren't meant to have a blah marriage or a ho-hum sex life. You are meant to enjoy your husband—and that means he's supposed to rock your world too!

The Celebration

Marriage is all about becoming one. But that "becoming" is a process—it doesn't happen overnight. Sure, it may happen instantaneously in God's eyes, but it usually takes time and effort for us mortals to truly feel "one": to truly become intertwined in every sense of the word.

In my focus group with husbands, one made an interesting comment: "When you're one, sex becomes a part of that, and you lose all the shyness you had at the beginning of marriage. Now we can do a whole lot more because it's not dirty; it's just expressing who we are together, and we're so much more comfortable."

Becoming one and feeling spiritually connected did not mean that their love life became more chaste; rather, it became more adventurous and fun and, at the same time, more comfortable and natural.

Experiencing that spiritual connection during sex doesn't happen simply by doing typically "sacred" things in the bedroom; it is done by recognizing that the sex life you share is already sacred. Isn't that what God wants—to take more and more into his sphere? And as you grow closer together, you're able to grow in freedom together so that more is holy and right between you, even if it's also hot.

Getting the physical side of marriage right may take some work, but it's a fun kind of work. And with the right attitude, we women can become the happiest wives who are married to the most satisfied husbands. That's what God wants for us, and that's what he'll help you do once you start getting excited about it. So jump in! Sex can be relaxing, intimate, and stupendous all at the same time. Commit to having a marriage that is on fire: not just for your husband but for you too. You are a beautiful creature. You were created for this. So, dear friends, go grab your husbands and have some fun.

How to Have an Amazing Honeymoon

A few weeks before my wedding, I bought a bestselling Christian sex book. I read it cover to cover while sitting in the bathtub. Instead of helping me feel confident about my wedding night, it left me a nervous wreck. And a little angry.

First, it was all about the mechanics of sex. The book's focus was on making sure that you, the woman, had an orgasm on your first sexual encounter. It went through everything you were supposed to do and everything he was supposed to do in explicit detail, complete with a time schedule. After reading the book and raging at it, I drowned it. I stuffed it under the water and held it there until it died, and then I unceremoniously dumped it in the garbage.

Let me try to explain why I felt so homicidal toward a book. I didn't like feeling as if my every action was prescribed. I didn't want sex to feel choreographed. I didn't want to feel like there was a right way to do it. But perhaps most importantly, I didn't want the night to be so stressful that it could be measured based on whether I had "succeeded." What if I simply wanted to be comfortable with my husband and have fun exploring rather than trying to force my body to do something?

Given that that particular book sold over 2,500,000 copies, I'm sure it has helped many women enjoy their wedding nights.[1] But there is a trend in Christian thinking that goes something like this: *the wedding night is the big night you've been waiting for your whole life, so you had better do everything right, or you will ruin it.*

A lot of pressure, isn't it?

Perhaps I'm a party pooper. Perhaps that book was right, and we should all aim for physical bliss. So I tested my own hypothesis. I took a survey of married Christian women, some of whom had waited for the wedding to be sexually active and some of whom had made love before, and I asked them to rate the sex on their wedding night.

I discovered that despite selling many copies, the book's message hadn't succeeded in making wedding nights more explosive. Of the women in my survey who didn't have sex before marriage, only 16 percent reached orgasm on their wedding night through intercourse. Another 14 percent reached it another way, but 70 percent didn't experience orgasm at all. In fact, even among those who'd had sex before, in no category did over 50 percent of women reach orgasm on the night they were married. It simply isn't that common.

Here's the way I see it: fireworks are great. But the point of the wedding night is that it's a *wedding* night. The bliss is that you're now together in every way. You can now explore, have fun, and discover all on your own time. For some people, that's going to mean fireworks right off the bat. For others it may take longer. But it doesn't matter because now you're finally married, and you have decades to get it right.

We can look at that paltry 16 percent figure and conclude,

"Wow, we need to educate people more about how to have sex so that more women can have orgasms on their wedding night." Or we can say, "Maybe for most people sex is a fun learning curve, not an instantaneous achievement. And that's okay." Personally, I like the second option.

Make the wonder of the wedding night about getting to know your husband in new and exciting ways and not about reaching some sort of physical milestone. Otherwise it becomes so, well, *serious*. And who wants to be serious on their wedding night?

C. S. Lewis, in his book *The Four Loves*, wrote, "Banish play and laughter from the bed of love and you may let in a false goddess."[2] Sex is funny. Our body parts are funny. It's a little messy, a little quirky, and often awkward. But it's fun. And if we make an orgasm something we have to achieve *or else*, we lose the fun.

So let's take a more relaxed but realistic look at what the honeymoon is likely to be. Some of you are newbies at this whole making love thing. You've never done it before, and you're gearing up for your first encounter. Others of you have been sexually active, but you likely still want to make the wedding night meaningful. Whichever group you're in, let's look together at how to begin this journey to great wedded sex.

Planning Ahead for a Great Honeymoon

First, some practicalities that can't be overlooked.

Plan Birth Control (or Lack of It)

If you're getting married, you need to plan whether you want to be parents right away. Give some thought to birth control early—months before the wedding, if possible—because many methods require a lead time. In chapter 2 we looked at birth control methods, including choosing none at all. This is a crucial decision that you should talk to your fiancé about now.

Book a Checkup

Whether you're walking down the aisle as a sexual novice or you've had plenty of experience, a trip to the doctor before the wedding can help you get off to a reassuring start to your married life.

I'll talk to the sexual novices first. Talking to your physician about your plan for birth control is certainly beneficial. Also, doctors are in the business of assuming something could be wrong, so he or she will likely want to do an internal exam to make sure you're healthy. That exam consists of you lying on an examining table with your feet in stirrups while the physician inserts a speculum inside you, which looks a bit like a hair straightener. Once the speculum is all the way in, the doctor will open it so that he or she can swab your cervix (the opening to your uterus). Then he or she will remove the speculum, exchange it for a couple of fingers, and feel around to ensure that everything is in the right place and the right size and shape.

I'm not a doctor, so I can't give you medical advice, but here's what I will say. Talk to your doctor about the need for the exam before you acquiesce to it. The doctor is looking primarily for cervical cancer, and the sexually transmitted disease human papillomavirus (HPV) causes over 90 percent of cervical cancers. If you haven't been sexually active, your risk of cervical cancer is miniscule. And if you've been having regular periods, with normal amounts of cramping, the chances of something being physically wrong that requires immediate treatment is also slim.

Speaking as a woman who, thirty years into marriage, still has to hum and "go to my happy place" to get through an internal exam, I wouldn't recommend it unless your doctor says it's essential or unless you want reassurance that you're normal and healthy. Perhaps your physician will agree that there isn't an immediate need for an internal exam. If you do go ahead with one, ask the doctor to go slowly, to make sure you are comfortable, and, if possible, to use an adolescent speculum.

On the other hand, if you've been sexually active before, have the full exam—and the battery of tests for sexually transmitted diseases. You don't want to pass something along, and you want to start your marriage with complete honesty. Physicians are also accustomed to helping people deal with STIs that have long-term effects, such as herpes. Your physician can help you learn to tell when herpes is dormant and what to do if it's not.

If the tests come back positive for any STI, you'll likely experience a period of grieving and shame. Talk to your fiancé about it, and be completely open with him. He loves you. He wants to marry you. The chances of that changing are slim, but if you keep this from him, you'll start your marriage on rocky ground.

And if your fiancé has been sexually active, ask him to have all the tests done too. Reassure him that no matter what the outcome, you will still love him and still want to marry him. After all, if you can't say that, you likely shouldn't be walking down the aisle in the first place.

Now that we've dealt with the medical details, let's focus on how to plan for the wedding night.

Think Exhaustion

The most common regret women completing my survey reported about their wedding night was plain and simple exhaustion. If you're up at six in the morning the day of your wedding to dress, head to the hairdresser, apply your makeup, pose for pictures, get married, take more pictures, host the reception, and then dance until midnight, how alert and energetic do you think you'll be once you're back at the hotel room?

Listen to these warnings from survey respondents:

I wish I'd left the party earlier so I'd have more energy.

....

As awful as this sounds, I was so exhausted on my wedding night, I didn't even want to have sex.

....

We had to help clean up after the wedding. Then drop a few
relatives off on the way to our hotel. We got to the hotel at two
in the morning. Needless to say, we showered and went straight
to sleep!

....

Got to the hotel still all dolled up, flopped on the bed as shoes
went flying, woke up the next morning pretty much exactly as
we fell asleep. Holding hands, still all dolled up.

If you want maximum energy at night, schedule an early ceremony. If you have to fly for your honeymoon and the airport is a
distance away, take a day together in a hotel before you leave. Don't
force yourself to drive for a few hours after your wedding or schedule yourself to wake up at five in the morning to catch your plane.
Think relaxation. You want to be able to lounge in bed with your
hubby. Don't make unrealistic plans that sound fun in theory but
will actually be exhausting!

On the other hand, maybe dancing until 2:00 a.m. is important
to you. Maybe you do want to take off for Jamaica at dawn the next
morning. If these are priorities for you, that's fine. But be realistic
about your expectations, and consider postponing that first sexual
encounter until you are rested and relaxed.

One other bit of advice from our survey takers: lay off alcohol
at the reception. For many newlyweds, and especially the younger
ones, alcohol hasn't been a big part of their lives. Now is not the
time to see what having three glasses of wine feels like. Stay away
from heavy alcohol indulgence, and encourage your husband to do
so as well. A full 10 percent of our wedding night survey respondents didn't make love that first night because their husbands passed
out or because they were too tipsy. Definitely not a highlight for a
wedding night.

Think Memorable

Many women who completed my survey also reported putting a lot of thought into the wedding but very little into the honeymoon. They felt selfish or wasteful spending too much money on a vacation, so they poured it all into the ceremony. But allocating some of the wedding budget to a nice hotel room is wise. Quite a few survey respondents expressed appreciation for their Jacuzzi tubs! And when you plan your honeymoon, plan something to do. You probably won't have sex 24/7. You'll want to go for a walk, play golf, swim, sightsee, or something else you enjoy. Book accordingly.

Think Period

You hoped against hope it wouldn't happen, but it did. Your wedding day arrives, and so does your period. You have to wear a white dress all day, and it feels like your plans for the night are ruined.

If you have enough time leading up to your wedding, a little planning can make this scenario less likely. Keep track of your cycles as soon as you can. You can make educated guesses about six to eight months out about when you'll likely have your period. And then try to schedule your wedding smack in the middle, so that even if you miscalculate by a week or so, it won't matter.

If, after all your best planning, your period comes anyway, cry about it for a few minutes and then try to let it go. In the broader scheme of life, it won't matter much. Decide instead to make your honeymoon into a time where you can get to know each other and have fun outside the bedroom. And in the bedroom, he can focus on other parts of your body rather than your vagina, and if you're comfortable with it, you can ask him to show you how to bring him to orgasm another way (since he will probably be rather eager to do *something*). Don't consider it a failure; have fun doing what you can, and know the rest will come in time.

Think Lingerie

I've heard it said that lingerie is the most expensive item of clothing once the amount of time we wear it is factored in, since we tend to have it on for only a few seconds before it's tossed aside. But it's the effect that counts. Besides, you'll likely feel far more confident in something—even if it's barely anything—than you will naked. So bring something cute. But not *just* lingerie. Here are the brutal facts: lingerie doesn't cover much, and hotels can be on the chilly side. Pack some regular pajamas too.

But don't be scared of being naked. Your husband will want to see your whole body—all of it. That can be scary if you haven't been sexually active because chances are few people have seen you naked before. Even if you're not new at this, if most of your sexual encounters have been rather quick, you may never have been fully gazed at before.

He'll likely want to gaze. And that's good.

Even if you're a little nervous, try to drink it in. Realize how much he loves your body. It's like you're one big playground for him, and he will adore your body, no matter what it looks like. If you can calm down, relax, and revel in how much he enjoys you, you'll feel more sexually confident. Most of us are insecure about our bodies. Instead of focusing on your feelings, watch how he feels. Notice the effect you have on him. That's all you, honey. He finds you attractive. He finds you beautiful. Start believing it about yourself too.

And while you're at it—have fun gazing at him! It may feel awkward at first, and often gazing at him in a bathtub or shower is easier. But you're allowed to look at him and enjoy him, so revel in him!

Think Lubricant

Sex is much easier if you're well lubricated (if your vagina is slippery). It makes it easier for your husband's penis to enter and makes it far more comfortable for you when he thrusts. When women are aroused, our bodies naturally produce fluids to keep us "wet." But when we're nervous, lubrication isn't easy to achieve. So bring some lubricant with you. You may not need it, but it's good to have it just in case.

Think Boundaries

Okay, all that practical info aside, the big question I get from most engaged women is, "Is it a sin if we have sex before the wedding?"

Can I stir the pot a little bit here? What if "Is it a sin" is the wrong question? I think these are better questions: "How can I live out the kingdom of God with my fiancé and do what reflects Christ's ways? How can we do what is wise?" We often frame sex before marriage primarily as a sin issue, where God will love us if we wait and will be angry if we don't. I do believe that God's intention is that we reserve sex for marriage, but I think that's because he's a protective God who wants our best.

God made sex for multiple reasons: to have babies, to help us feel close to each other, and to feel great. All of these are better in marriage. Practically, marriage ensures that any children who come along are part of a lifelong relationship where they can be cared for. As well, when you commit to each other in marriage before having sex, the sexual relationship benefits from the foundation of an emotional and spiritual connection that is already there. Couples who have sex early in their relationship may *feel* strongly that they are connected because of those bonding hormones and having shared such an intimate experience. But one can mistake sexual intimacy for emotional intimacy and gloss over gaping holes in other areas of a relationship, failing to realize how shallow it is. In contrast, when you delay sex till after marriage, you naturally spend the lead-up time growing closer to each other emotionally and spiritually and building a strong friendship. Sex alone can't hold a marriage together. You will need that emotional and spiritual connection.

That's not to say waiting won't be difficult; it probably will be. And it *should* be. If you love him and feel close to him, you will naturally want to have sex with him. Take appropriate measures to make it easier rather than harder to resist those impulses. Try not to be alone together too late at night or hang out lying down on a bed. But remember that rules alone can't help you withstand temptation. This has to be a decision you make together with good reasons—so that you can grow other parts of your relationship before marriage, so that you can foster self-control, and so that you can be sure this is the right person for you.

Thoughts for Sexually Active Couples

When Natalie was dating her now-husband, she knew he'd had sex with other women before. She loved him and wanted to keep him and figured that he expected sex with her. So they became sexually active.

Maybe in your relationship you're already sexually active too. I'm going to suggest something radical: consider stopping until the wedding. You may figure, "What's the point? The horse has already left the barn." But it's not about whether you've had sex in the past; it's about what you choose to do *today*.

When you decide to stop having sex, you show each other that your relationship is what's keeping you together, not just the fireworks. And when you stop having sex, you also say, "I want to work on our intimacy and emotional connection, not just on sex. I want the foundation to be strong." And finally, you show him, and he shows you, "I am capable of waiting. I am capable of self-control." You'll need that assurance after you're married too. There will always be times when sex is off the table, like after childbirth or over work trips or during family crises or illnesses. Showing that you can love each other faithfully without sex, without turning to porn or other lovers, and without getting grumpy is an amazing gift.

What if he's not open to stopping until the wedding? Consider that a red flag. Someone who truly loves you will honor your boundaries. Besides, once you're married, he'll still need to practice self-control. If he can't do that for you now, he's unlikely to willingly do it later.

Disclose Your Sexual Past

Maybe you've had sex in the past, maybe he has, or perhaps both of you have. But "having a past" does not necessarily mar your future. I know many women who have married guys with sexual pasts (or vice versa), and it hasn't significantly impacted their marriage. I also know plenty of couples where one of them can't get over their spouse's past, and it continues to haunt them decades later. What puts some couples in the first category and some in the second?

Healthy couples deal with their baggage before marriage. They tell each other what they need to, but they reassure their beloved that it is in the past. How much do you reveal? A good rule of thumb is this: don't give enough detail that they could picture anything. Yes, it's important to know general numbers: Are we talking about one person? Five people? Dozens? It's important that they know the nature of the relationships: Were these long-term monogamous relationships? A series of hookups or one-night stands? And it's important to know the nature of the sexual encounters: Were they coerced? Was sexual assault involved? Or were they consensual?

If sexual assault or promiscuity was a part of your story or his, seek out a licensed counselor and work through anything that needs to be dealt with. Often promiscuity is a trauma response and may signal that something else is going on that needs to be looked at. Full recovery doesn't always happen before marriage, especially when trauma is involved. But it's important to be on a good trajectory and to go into marriage with your eyes open—and with wise counsel.

Your fiancé also deserves to know if porn use is a part of your past—or your present. And believe me, you need to know if porn is a part of his life too. Every day on my blog, women pour out their stories to me of discovering a husband's porn use years after marriage and how devastating that is. Porn habits have one of the most toxic impacts on a couple's sex life, *and marriage will not cure a porn addiction.* But porn use doesn't necessarily doom your sex life; many guys use porn but put it behind them and recover. Nevertheless, both of you should be free of porn for at least a few months before you walk down the aisle, and there should be accountability in place so you're confident that it is, indeed, over.

Finally, don't marry someone if you can't accept their sexual past. None of us is perfect. When you say those vows, you promise to love each other completely, and that includes who they are despite—or even because of—their past. If you can't accept that, it is unfair to marry him and then hold it over his head as if he robbed you of something. Either marry him wholeheartedly, or leave him the freedom to marry someone who can.

What's Sex like the First Time?

A few years ago Keith and I were speaking at a marriage conference in Atlantic Canada, where we conducted a session with the six engaged couples who had joined the hundreds of married ones. Keith talked to the men; I talked to the women. The men were mostly interested in learning how to wait until the wedding night. The women were far more interested in the technical side: "Does it hurt?" "If I can't use a tampon, does that mean I can't have sex?" "What's the hymen?" Women are far more physically vulnerable during intercourse than men are, and it impacts us more than it does them! So let's go over these concerns in detail to put your mind at ease.

Think Big

Men may worry about whether their penises are large enough, but the first time a woman sees an erect penis, she's often surprised at its size. After you've squeezed a few babies out, it may not seem so huge, but when all you have to compare it to is a tampon, it's big. But don't worry, it fits. Really. Your vagina is designed to stretch and usually feels good when it does. You'll get used to it and come to like it.

Think Messy

Showering before you make love—if you're not too eager to jump into bed—can make the whole experience more pleasant. After all, if you're arriving at your honeymoon suite after a three-hour dance, chances are you're both pretty sweaty. Showering can make kissing and touching his body a more attractive proposition.

But even with a shower, sex can be messy! When your husband reaches orgasm, especially if he hasn't ejaculated for a while, he releases a lot of semen inside you (unless he's using a condom). Combine that with the natural fluids that women produce when we're sexually excited, and quite a puddle can form that is no fun to sleep on later that night. Stick a towel or some tissue by the bed to wipe up afterward or to put underneath you when you make love.

On television couples always snuggle after making love. They don't ever get up and do something so mundane as going to the bathroom. But it's a good idea for both of you to head to the toilet afterward. Urinating afterward reduces the chances of urinary tract infections (UTIs). And that's something important to keep at the back of your mind because a burst of sexual activity can all too easily lead to a UTI or a yeast infection.

Not to give too much information here, but the few times I've had a UTI have been after anniversary weekends when my husband and I escaped by ourselves and rarely left the bedroom. Then when we landed back home, all of a sudden I felt like I had just downed three Big Gulps on my way to visit Niagara Falls. As I've mentioned before, my husband is a pediatrician, and he works in our local emergency room. When a doctor you personally know asks, "So have you done anything different or out of the ordinary lately?" it can be awkward.

Do your best to avoid unfortunate medical visits. UTIs are caused by germs entering the urethra. If you take antibiotics for a UTI, the antibiotics kill off all the good bacteria in your body. The lack of good bacteria can lead to a yeast infection, causing itchiness and discomfort in your genital area, which leads to more treatments. It can be a vicious cycle.

But never fear! As long as you take a few simple precautions, you will likely avoid these two issues. Both you and your husband should urinate after each sexual encounter because, as weird as it sounds, pee is sterile. It cleans everything out. Also, make sure your husband washes his genital area every day so no germs are transferred (though he doesn't have to rush to the shower before sex each time).

There's no need to become paranoid about these issues, though. Our vaginas are self-cleaning. You don't need to buy feminine wash products, because they can often throw off your healthy bacteria balance and lead to more problems. Go to the bathroom a lot, take probiotics, and for extra caution, bring along some cranberry juice and yogurt.

Does It Hurt?

The book that I drowned said that first-time sex won't hurt if you do everything right. That sure wasn't true for me! Here are a few comments to set the record straight:

"The first time doesn't hurt."

"It is sooo painful."

Guess that didn't clear the issue up much, did it? I suppose we should conclude that the correct answer is, "It depends."

Most women experience at least a slight sting when the hymen, the layer of skin that partially covers the opening of the vagina, tears. If you're aroused, it's not that it doesn't hurt, but you probably just won't care! But any pain is usually abrupt, and then it's over. Some women bleed, and some don't. Stash a towel nearby to protect the sheets and you'll be fine either way. If you don't bleed, it doesn't mean you didn't do it right. Some women tear their hymens earlier in life without realizing it. It also doesn't mean you weren't a virgin. It just means that you're blessed with less pain!

Before I was married, a close friend who had been wed for a year told me that she was quite surprised at how sex in the "missionary position," with him on top, stopped hurting pretty quickly, but over the next few days, whenever they tried new positions, the pain returned. It makes sense. Your body isn't used to intercourse, and stretching your vagina in ways it hasn't been stretched before can make you sore. But the pain will likely go away, and if something hurts too much, don't try that position right now.

If you find that the pain is more intense, then you may have muscle pain rather than hymen pain. That's usually because you're having a hard time relaxing, and when you're tense, the muscles at the top one and a half inches of your vagina (closest to the opening) can tense involuntarily (or, in certain cases, the muscles farther up). Here's what to do: Ask your husband to stop moving once he's inside you (if you can manage this). Tense your muscles as hard as you can around his penis, and then relax deliberately. That can cause the involuntary muscle spasm to stop. Do that for a few minutes, and usually the problem goes away.

Here's what one woman said about difficulties with penetration: "My husband was a virgin as well and was very patient with me despite being excited. When I couldn't relax enough to allow for penetration, he suggested waiting until the next day and cuddling. The next day we were both rested from our large wedding, and we were able to have intercourse. It was great!"

Some couples do take a few days, or even a week, before penetration is comfortable. If it's difficult, don't try repeatedly. Take a hiatus, have some fun in other ways, and circle back in a day or two. Instead of having intercourse, learn to bring each other to orgasm in other ways first, which also helps you get more familiar with each other's bodies. And most women who experience some pain at first find that it resolves in a few days. So seriously—don't panic! Remember, if you are tense about being tense, it will only make you more tense. Give it a little time to see if you simply need to relax. After all, you've been through one of the most stressful and busiest periods of your life. You may just need space to breathe again.

You don't have to have intercourse right away, and you certainly don't have to reach orgasm right out of the gate. Not everybody consummates their marriage on their wedding night. Whether it's because of exhaustion, your period, or even some pain, it may not happen for you. In our survey, about 15 percent of women didn't end up having sex on their wedding night. But that had no bearing on whether they enjoy sex today!

At the beginning of your sexual life together, allow your bodies to set the tempo, and go at the pace of the person who is least comfortable. This isn't a race. You're not medieval royalty where the wedding party is waiting outside the door to see the bloodied sheets. You have the privilege of getting to unwrap sex using the most natural timeline.

The Only Timeline You Need for Sex

And here it is: the *one* piece of advice I most want you to remember if you're beginning your sexual life together. Think of the natural order for great sex like this:

Feel comfortable → Reach arousal → Have intercourse

Too many couples start with step #3: *Have intercourse.* Starting there can feel uncomfortable, disappointing, and even bewildering. And then feeling comfortable and aroused can be difficult because it's almost like you're going backward! But if you can first aim for feeling comfortable, and then learn how your body reaches arousal (and even orgasm) before you start intercourse, you'll be on great footing for the rest of your marriage.

Hopefully once you're aroused, intercourse will naturally flow. But some women still feel nervous, and one thing that contributes to that hesitation is the idea that sex is something that happens "to" women—*he* is going to do something to *you*. No wonder sex can seem threatening! You may be one of those women who has no qualms about it at all, but if you do feel nervous, try to reframe the experience in your own mind.

Sex is something beautiful where you can truly share yourself—all of yourself—with someone who will love you forever. Instead of seeing sex as something he does to you, think of it as something you do together. To help put you in that mindset, take the lead in touching him and getting to know his body. If you're more active as a participant, not only a recipient, you can feel more empowered and sexual as you explore.

Finally, a word to those who try but find that intercourse is still painful or even impossible after a few days or weeks. Please see a physician. You may have a thicker hymen that needs to be surgically removed (which is rare), or you may suffer from vaginismus or another sexual pain disorder. I wish before we had walked down the aisle, I had been warned something like that could happen. Instead, it hit me out of the blue. I felt like I was broken, and I was desperate to prove that I could "do it," so I forced myself to have intercourse even though it hurt, just so that I could say we had done it. I wish that I had given myself a few days to get comfortable.

Now, don't be alarmed! *Most of you will not experience this.* Yes, our survey found that 22.6 percent of women suffer sexual pain not related to childbirth at some point, and around 7 percent of women experience it to the extent that penetration is impossible. But that means almost 80% do not! Understanding that sexual pain *can* occur, though, and even more importantly *why* it occurs, can actually make it less likely to happen to you—and more likely that, if it does, it will be something you can recover from quickly.

Avoiding Any Wedding Night Land Mines

One of the findings from our survey of twenty thousand women is that women who are virgins on their wedding day are 25.1 percent more likely to experience vaginismus than women who had sex with their now-husbands before the wedding.[3] After we talked to these women and asked some follow-up survey questions, one factor seems to be that they rush to intercourse because they feel like that's what they're supposed to do, skipping all the natural sexual progression steps that make her aroused. They don't follow the relaxed timeline.

Having sex for the first time on the wedding night also adds another complication: you're having sex *because you're supposed to.* Even if you want to, doing so "on demand" because you're supposed to can feel like you don't have a choice. The feeling that sex is something you *must* do, no matter what you feel like, is highly implicated in vaginismus.[4]

So, girls, reclaim your choice! Talk before the wedding about how this isn't a pass/fail test: you have a lot of time to figure this out. Some couples will get aroused and excited on the first night, and others may take a few days or even weeks. *But you'll end up in the same place.* If Keith and I had waited a few days until I was truly ready and didn't feel pressure, rather than plowing ahead, I believe we would have saved ourselves years of heartache—and that's the story the numbers tell too. Explore each other's bodies. Discover how each other works. Let him bring you to orgasm in another way before you attempt intercourse, using the steps in the physical section of this book, unless your body is shouting for him to enter you! That's abiding by the body's natural sexual progression rather than an artificial timeline about when to "do the deed," and it's more likely to work out well in the long run.

Think beyond the Wedding Night

We've gone over all the practical aspects of what to expect on the wedding night, but I feel a little bit like Paul at the end of 1 Corinthians 12. In that chapter, he outlined all the purposes and gifts in the church and how they're all vital. In chapter 14, he took up the same subject and went over decorum during worship. But in the middle of all these practicalities, he took a bit of a detour, announcing, "And yet I will show you the most excellent way" (12:31). And then he wrote that beautiful chapter on love.

And now, girls, I would like to show you a more excellent way too. And like Paul's more excellent way, this one has everything to do with love as well.

When you are married, your husband is a new person, and so are you. You are truly one flesh. No matter what your sexual experience, or lack thereof, this will be the first time you explore his body when it's not just his body—it's also yours! Make it meaningful. Consider praying before you make love to dedicate the sexual part of your relationship to God.

But let's get practical. How do you bring the emotional and relational elements into something that is so physically anticipated? It sounds mysterious, but I think it simply means paying attention to those areas of your relationship. Bring your friendship into it! Laugh together. Learn to be comfortable naked. Have a bath together. Touch each other. And remember that if things don't work perfectly now, it's okay because you're learning, and learning is good. Take some time out, laugh, and even play Scrabble or Monopoly naked together.

And how about feeling that spiritual connection? Kiss and memorize each other with your fingers, your eyes, your lips. You don't need to hurry. Use your senses to memorize his body—and encourage him to use his. Trace your fingers along his body with your eyes closed so that you can concentrate on what it feels like.

Do the same with your eyes open. Revel in the newfound discovery. And when you have intercourse, look into his eyes when he enters you. Remember to say, "I love you."

One last bit of reassurance: if you have a "bad" wedding night, when you're not particularly relaxed and you don't orgasm and sex is ho-hum at best, this experience has no bearing on the quality of your sex life later on. *Absolutely none.*

Don't believe me? Here are the numbers. Of the women who were virgins on their wedding night yet who orgasmed anyway, 65 percent rated their sex life today as great, 30 percent rated it as okay, and 5 percent rated it as awful. Among those who didn't orgasm at all, 64 percent rated their sex life today as great, 28 percent rated it as okay, and 8 percent rated it as awful—*virtually the same results.* Some women are nervous on their honeymoon, and some are not. Some are willing to experiment right away, and some can't. But it doesn't matter which group you're in; give yourself a few years of marriage and you'll end up in roughly the same place.

Maybe you will be one of the few who reaches orgasm on her wedding night through intercourse. But whether or not you do, you can still feel that oneness. You can hug and rejoice and explore. You can experience that first taste of beautiful intimacy when you can be naked together, which is wonderful in and of itself. That is the real celebration.

Discussion Questions

For Engaged Couples

This book comes with a companion book for your fiancé—*The Good Guy's Guide to Great Sex*! Ideally, have him read his book, and then, after you're both finished, set aside two or three blocks of time to discuss these questions together.

Preparing for Marriage

1. Does your partner know your sexual history? Take some time to share in general terms about how many partners you've had, whether those encounters have been in long- or short-term relationships, and whether they have been consensual or not. Allow your partner to ask any questions they have, but remember that you should not answer anything that might allow your partner to picture something explicitly. Talk about how you will put your sexual past (if any) behind you, and assure each other that the past is truly in the past.

2. Do you intend to use contraception? If so, each of you think of the method you are most drawn to, and then talk about this with each other. Do you have reservations about what your spouse wants to do? How will you decide what to do?
3. What do you want to do about sexual activity before the wedding? If you intend to wait for sex until you're married, make practical plans for how to make this easier. If you have been sexually active, does one or both of you want to stop? Are you honoring each other's boundaries?
4. Has porn or erotica been a part of your life? How much has this affected your view of sexuality? Is either a part of your life now? What are your plans to deal with this?
5. Have you experienced sexual abuse or other trauma in your past? Have you sought help and treatment for it? Your partner needs to be aware of any trauma you have suffered. If you have never disclosed this, please do so before the wedding. If there are any known triggers (like settings, sounds, touches, etc.), share them with your partner so you can be sensitive to each other and avoid them as much as possible.
6. Is there something that could affect your sex life that you need to seek help for before marriage? For instance, could you benefit from seeing a trauma therapist, going to a licensed counselor, or dealing with porn or other addictions? What plans do you have to adequately address any roadblocks before the wedding?

Planning for the Honeymoon/Wedding

7. Discuss your expectations for the wedding night. Are you both confident that you'll be able to go at the slower person's pace? How can you make sure that you aim for arousal on your honeymoon?

8. What is your main goal for your honeymoon? Do you want to experience a big adventure together, or do you want something more relaxed? Do you want to travel or stay closer to home? If sex will be new for you, is what you're planning conducive to getting used to sex? Talk about how to plan for a honeymoon that will be the most memorable while also helping you feel intimate, relaxed, and comfortable.

Planning for Romance

9. How are you going to keep having fun outside the bedroom once you're married? What things are you doing now while you're dating that you want to make sure you continue?

10. Each of you think of a time when your beloved did something that showed that they loved and cherished you. What about it made you feel special? Share that memory. How can you each bring more romance into your relationship?

Planning for Sex

11. For many couples, orgasm is a skill that takes a while to learn. How will you handle it if orgasm is difficult for you? What will you do to both bring down the pressure and also keep aiming for your pleasure?

12. Turn to the diagram for the sexual response cycle (p. 173). Do you understand the difference between excitement, arousal, and orgasm? Reassure each other that you will take the time and attention needed to go through each stage.

13. One of the key factors in women's orgasm is women feeling they can speak up during sex if something isn't working for them. Discuss: what is the best way that he can make

it easier for you to feel like you can speak up? Are there things that either of you are nervous about communicating during sex? How can you reassure each other that speaking up isn't a criticism, but a desire to move towards real passion? Commit to each other now that you will speak up during sex when things aren't going the way you want, and that you will respond positively to your partner if that happens.

14. Did you grow up hearing that sex is a duty that people need to perform in marriage? Have you believed this? How will you ensure that in your marriage sex will always be something mutual and never coerced or pressured? Talk about how you will handle each other's "no."

15. Are there things you would like your spouse to do that you think will help you feel loved and close during sex? Discuss these together.

For Married Couples

This book comes with a companion book for your husband—*The Good Guy's Guide to Great Sex*! Ideally, have him read his book, and then, after you're both finished, set aside two or three blocks of time to discuss these questions together.

Setting the Stage

1. God made sex to be intimate, mutual, and pleasurable for both. In which area do you think you're strongest as a couple? Which area do you think you struggle with most? Think about it individually and then compare answers. Discuss ways you can improve the areas you both feel need improvement (especially if they're different!).

2. Is there an area of your sex life where you might benefit from some outside help (from a doctor, a pelvic floor

physiotherapist, a licensed marriage counselor, a trauma-informed counselor, a porn recovery group)? What have been the barriers to getting that help? How can you overcome them?

Emotional Intimacy

3. What kind of touch warms you up and makes you more interested in sex? Are there kinds of touch that make you less interested? What would you like your spouse to do more of?

4. Each of you think of a time when your spouse did something that showed that they loved and cherished you. What about it made you feel special? Share that memory with your spouse. How can you each bring more romance into your relationship?

Physical Intimacy

5. Turn to the diagram for the sexual response cycle (p. 173). Are there steps you feel you may have been skipping or rushing through too quickly? Discuss ways to make sex feel as good as possible for both of you.

6. Are you both regularly reaching orgasm? If not, discuss how you will make the person who is not reaching orgasm a priority in your lovemaking. Are there certain positions or types of stimulation that are more likely to lead to orgasm? Women often feel self-conscious if orgasm takes too long or isn't happening. Is this a problem for you? If so, how will you address it? Men are sometimes defensive if they're asked to do different things in bed to stimulate her. Is this a problem for you? If so, how will you address it?

7. During a sexual encounter, do you each feel comfortable communicating with your spouse in the moment if something isn't working or you want something different?

If not, identify the barriers that keep you from doing so. Is there something you or your spouse can do to make this easier?

Spiritual Intimacy

8. When you're making love, do you feel emotionally close to your spouse? How can you enhance your emotional connection during sex?

9. Share with your spouse your favorite sexual memory. What was it about that encounter that was so amazing? What can you do to create more sexual memories?

10. Are there things you would like to do to spice up the bedroom? Talk openly to each other about your ideas. Remember the principles in the book about how adding spice is meant to enhance intimacy, not detract from it, and honor each other's "no."

11. Do you feel comfortable stopping a sexual encounter if it's not working for you? How can you and your spouse set up a dynamic where both of you feel free to initiate or to stop things without any fear or guilt? Do you ever have sex only out of obligation? What can you each do to change this dynamic so that sex is something you each enter enthusiastically? (If coercion is ever a part of your sexual life, please seek help.)

Libido

12. What are your top three libido killers? Guess your spouse's and compare notes. What can you each do to reduce your spouse's libido killers?

13. Do you have a spontaneous or responsive libido? What do you think your spouse has? Compare answers. Of the two of you, does one of you want sex more? Does one want it less? How can you make sure you're making each

other feel wanted and desired based on the principles in this book?

14. Out of the last five times you made love, who initiated: him, her, or both of you? Compare your answers. Are you happy with this, or do you want to make some changes?

Acknowledgments

I have been chomping at the bit to rewrite *The Good Girl's Guide to Great Sex* for a few years now, ever since we did our huge survey of twenty thousand women. So I am indebted to Carolyn McCready at Zondervan, who convinced others that, even though the original was selling well, it was still worth revamping! I'm so happy with how it turned out. I know this was a huge investment of time and energy that Zondervan wasn't anticipating when they hired us to write *The Good Guy's Guide to Great Sex*, but having the two books as companions, both up to date and accessible, is something I'm so excited about.

My agent, Chip MacGregor, originally convinced Zondervan to take a chance on me ten years ago when I was still an unknown little Canadian. Chip, you've got incredible persuasion skills, and I'm so glad that we paired up at Write Canada all those years ago. You've become a good friend and a tremendous advocate for my work. Thank you.

I'm very grateful to Joanna Sawatsky, my stats expert and dear friend, who took a look at the original surveys I did for the original edition of this book and pronounced them "actually not that bad." But I'm very glad that we could add surveys that are pretty darn amazing, and that's all due to Joanna, who actually knows how to calculate odds ratios and p values and chi squares. Speaking of data, a special thank you to the twenty thousand women who took our horrendously long Bare Marriage Survey (seriously, it was like half an hour of their lives, which adds up to ten thousand hours, or 416 days). And a thank you to the three thousand guys who took our even more invasive survey! You guys are awesome, and I'm sorry some of the questions were so awkward.

Now, true confession: like most of my books and pretty much all of my podcasts, the best lines tend to be from my daughter Rebecca Lindenbach. Every morning when we go for walks with her son, Becca helps me talk through the arguments I'm trying to make and often creates soundbites way better than I ever could.

And thank you to copyeditor Kim Tanner for all your hard work, including wading through all the statistics. You took some of the confusing stuff and made it so much clearer. I appreciate it.

Thank you so much to our team on the Bare Marriage blog: my son-in-law Connor Lindenbach, who runs the technical side; my daughter Katie Emmerson, who edits the *Bare Marriage* podcast; my friend Emily Murchison, who helps with social media; and of course my friend Tammy Arseneau, who basically manages our lives. I appreciate you all so much. And to Elizabeth Wray, my mom, who lives with us and tries to make my life as easy as possible when I'm in work mode—I see it and appreciate it, even if I don't say it often enough.

I want to say a special shout-out to several people who have informed the way I think about sexuality, especially Andrew J. Bauman and Michael John Cusick. I also appreciate Emily Nagoski's work about the female sexual response cycle, which helped me use different words when we talk about libido. Sarah McDugal and Gretchen Baskerville have been so helpful in educating me about betrayal trauma and abuse, and I hope I did them proud in this book by including their perspectives to protect women who may be in dangerous relationships.

Thank you to the team at FamilyLife Canada, which has always encouraged us.

And thank you so much to my husband, Keith. When I first

brought up writing the companion book for this one, *The Good Guy's Guide to Great Sex*, with me, I know he was hesitant. He started speaking at marriage conferences when he wasn't sure about it; he started speaking on podcasts with me when he was nervous; he even started writing blog posts. And now he's written a book, and it turned out even better than either of us expected. He's an incredible editor, and I'm glad we found a new rhythm as we work together!

And finally, thank you to all our online social media followers and commenters who challenge me and encourage me. To all of our Bare Marriage Patreon supporters too, it is wonderful to have you to run our ideas off of before we put them to paper. Thank you for cheering us on as we wrote for women and for championing us as we decided to write for men too. You all keep me going, and I hope this book makes a difference in your lives, as you have all influenced how I write and see sex. I look forward to catching up on your comments every morning and appreciate you more than I can express.

Notes

Chapter 1: The Three Ingredients of Great Sex

1. One sample test for proportion, z>1.96. Results for each term are shown in the chart on p. 28.

2. Linda Waite and Maggie Gallagher, *The Case for Marriage: Why Married People Are Happier, Healthier, and Better Off Financially* (New York: Broadway, 2001). The discussion about commitment, sexual satisfaction, religion, and attitudes toward sex is found on pages 86–96.

3. Personal interview conducted on behalf of *Faith Today* magazine, December 2004.

4. Thomas Aquinas, *Summa Theologica*, question 49, "Of the Marriage Goods," article 2.

5. See Genesis 2:18: "The LORD God said, 'It is not good for the man to be alone. I will make a helper suitable for him.'" The Hebrew word for "helper" does not have a connotation of subordination, since it is used of God frequently in the Psalms. It does have a military connotation—God is our help and our shield.

Chapter 2: Great Sex Basics

1. Vincenzo Puppo and Ilan Gruenwald, "Does the G-Spot Exist? A Review of the Current Literature," *International Urogynecology Journal* 23 (June 2012): 1665–669, https://doi.org/10.1007/s00192 -012-1831-y. The reason that the region generally associated with the "G-spot" seems to be more pleasurable for women is likely related to the fact that when a woman has her pelvis tilted, other

anatomical areas press against her vaginal wall, putting pressure on the upper vaginal wall. It is also now believed that the clitoris has "roots" that extend upward, and these are stimulated when pressure is put on the front of the vaginal wall. This pressure may also be why women who report having sex when they feel a slight need to urinate report higher degrees of pleasure—the bladder is pushing down in that direction.

2. If you experience a great deal of pain at ovulation, please see a physician. Some cysts can cause pain, as can some other disorders, and often these can be dealt with quite easily.

3. In rare cases, a fertilized egg can implant in the fallopian tubes, causing an ectopic pregnancy that is life-threatening. If you ever feel intense pain when you might be pregnant, please see a doctor.

4. For example, the Billings Ovulation Method: https://billings.life/en/.

5. Though there has been controversy in the past, medical consensus is that the hormonal birth control methods do prevent ovulation. Some have worried that the pill prevents implantation but may still allow fertilization, but it does appear that ovulation is prevented. In addition, even if ovulation occurred, the pill also increases cervical mucous, which would prohibit sperm from entering the uterus and fertilizing the egg, thus preventing conception.

6. Zlatko Pastor, Katerina Holla, and Roman Chmel, "The Influence of Combined Oral Contraceptives on Female Sexual Desire: A Systematic Review," *The European Journal of Contraception & Reproductive Health Care* 18, no. 1 (2013): 27–43, https://doi.org/10.3109/13625187.2012.728643.

7. "Study: Copper IUDs Do Not Appear to Prevent Implantation or Increase HIV Risk," Relias Media, July 1, 2020, https://www.reliasmedia.com/articles/146320-study-copper-iuds-do-not-appear-to-prevent-implantation-or-increase-hiv-risk.

Chapter 4: Reaching for the Stars

1. We excluded men who suffer from erectile dysfunction from our sample, to arrive at the 47 point orgasm gap. The 95 percent figure for men almost always or always reaching orgasm is the same as

other large scale studies, including, for instance, D. A. Frederick et al., "Differences in Orgasm Frequency among Gay, Lesbian, Bisexual, and Heterosexual Men and Women in a U.S. National Sample," *Archives of Sexual Behavior* 47, (2018): 273–88, https://doi.org/10.1007/s10508 -017-0939-z).

2. This conclusion is based on the original survey that was conducted for the first edition of *The Good Girl's Guide to Great Sex*, of just shy of three thousand women, rather than the more recent survey. In the more recent one, we asked about age but not years married, so we cannot make a direct comparison. We believe that the drop off in sexual satisfaction around year twenty-five is likely due to the onset of menopause, which can make arousal more difficult for some women.

3. Global differences in orgasm rate by age were statistically significant using the chi-squared test for independence. Furthermore, residuals showed that each of the crosstabs included was statistically different from the expected count.

4. If you have trouble getting rid of some of these mental roadblocks, I encourage you to check out *The Great Sex Rescue: The Lies You Believed and How to Recover What God Intended*.

5. D. A. Frederick et al., "Differences in Orgasm Frequency among Gay, Lesbian, Bisexual, and Heterosexual Men and Women in a U.S. National Sample," *Archives of Sexual Behavior* 47, (2018): 273–88, https://doi.org/10.1007/s10508 -017-0939-z.

6. Practicing cutting off the flow of urine helps you identify your pelvic floor muscles so you can learn to control them better. But you shouldn't do this every time you pee, or you run the risk of urinary tract infections because you may fail to completely empty your bladder. So try these exercises to identify the muscles, but once you've identified them, try the exercises when you're not urinating.

Chapter 5: Learning to Make Love, Not Just Have Sex

1. Jennifer Degler, "Reader Question of the Week: What Can I Do If I Check Out during Sex Due to Childhood Sexual Abuse?,"

JenniferDegler.com, January 28, 2011, https://www.jenniferdegler
.com/checking-out-during-sex-due-to-childhood-sexual-abuse/.

2. Degler, "Reader Question of the Week."

3. Samuel L. Perry and Cyrus Schleifer, "Till Porn Do Us Part? A Longitudinal Examination of Pornography Use and Divorce," *Journal of Sex Research* 55, no. 3 (2018): 284–96, https://doi.org /10.1080/00224499.2017.1317709.

4. Ian Kerner, "Too Much Internet Porn: The SADD Effect," askmen, accessed September 28, 2021, http://ca.askmen.com/dating/love _tip_500/566_too-much-internet-porn-the-sadd-effect.html. Note: This is *not* a Christian resource, but I include it to show that secular counselors, despite years of recommending that couples watch porn together to reignite their sex life, are now admitting that it has negative effects, especially on men's libidos and abilities to respond sexually to their wives.

5. Andrew J. Bauman, "A Pornographic Style of Relating," AndrewJBauman.com, October 1, 2016, https://andrewjbauman .com/a-pornographic-style-of-relating.

6. Michael John Cusick, *Surfing for God* (Nashville: Nelson, 2012), 17.

7. From a personal conversation, October 20, 2021. You can find Sarah McDugal at https://wildernesstowild.com.

8. Andrew J. Bauman, "What Is a Sexually Healthy Man?," Andrewjbauman.com, October 26, 2020, https://andrewjbauman .com/waht-is-a-sexually-healthy-man.

9. Dr. Phil, "Actor Terry Crews on How an Addiction to Porn Almost Cost Him His Marriage," Dr. Phil YouTube Channel, March 14, 2018, https://youtu.be/ei0stwoEwOc.

10. Rebecca Crews, "No Sex for 90 Days?? The Sex Fast, Part 1," Terry Crews, March 7, 2016, YouTube video, 8:13, https://www.youtube .com/watch?v=tRCzTJ4gCKo.

11. Terry Crews, "No Sex for 90 Days?? The Sex Fast, Part 1," Terry Crews, March 7, 2016, YouTube video, 8:13, https://www.youtube .com/watch?v=tRCzTJ4gCKo.

Chapter 6: A Pure, Holy, and Hot Marriage

1. John Donne, *John Donne: The Major Works* (Oxford: Oxford University Press, 2000), 177.
2. C. S. Lewis, *The Lion, the Witch and the Wardrobe* (New York: HarperTrophy, 1994), 200.
3. Having sexual pleasure or a sexual response does not mean the encounter was consensual. "Arousal nonconcordance" is the phenomenon where your body and brain are not aligned with each other. One's body can become aroused and even reach orgasm even if the brain is telling you that you don't want this.
4. If you wonder if you're a victim of marital rape and coercion, please see my book *The Great Sex Rescue*. Other books that can be helpful are *Boundaries in Marriage* and *The Emotionally Destructive Marriage*.

Chapter 7: Becoming Best Friends

1. C. S. Lewis, *The Four Loves* (Glasgow: William Collins & Sons, 1960), 92.
2. CBS News, "Survey: One in Four Too Tired to Have Sex," March 10, 2010, https://www.cbsnews.com/news/survey-one-in-four-too-tired-to-have-sex/.
3. Eve Rodsky, *Fair Play* (New York: G.P. Putnam's Sons, 2019), 11.
4. To learn more about this concept, read *The Five Love Languages* by Gary Chapman (Chicago: Northfield, 2010), or use his assessment tool at https://www.5lovelanguages.com/quizzes.
5. Gwyneth Rees, "Parents Lose Two Months of Sleep in Baby's First Year," *Daily Mail Online*, March 29, 2007, http://www.dailymail.co.uk/news/article-445326/Parents-lose-months-sleep-babys-year.html.
6. The American Academy of Pediatrics reports that the risk of sudden infant death syndrome (SIDS) is substantially higher in cosleeping families. Read their report at "SIDS and Other Sleep-Related Infant Deaths: Updated 2016 Recommendations for a Safe Infant Sleeping Environment," *Pediatrics* 135, no. 5 (November 2016): e20162938, https://www.doi.org/10.1542/peds.2016-2938.

Chapter 8: From Fizzle to Sizzle for Her

1. Actual finding was 25.1 percent. The number was rounded for ease of reading.
2. Marital rape is illegal in most jurisdictions. And coercion occurs when bad things happen to the woman if she doesn't give sexual favors, whether it's the husband treating her or the children badly; withholding finances, communication, or other necessities; or quoting Scripture about obedience or submission. If you are in this sort of marriage, and you are in danger, please call a domestic abuse hotline. If you are not in immediate danger, please talk to a licensed counselor trained in abuse dynamics.
3. Personal conversation with Dr. Carol Peters-Tanksley, January 17, 2017, in Austin, Texas.
4. Anke Hambach et al., "The Impact of Sexual Activity on Idiopathic Headaches: An Observational Study," *Cephalalgia* 33, no. 6 (April 2013): 384–89, https://doi.org/10.1177/0333102413476374.

Chapter 9: From Fizzle to Sizzle for Him

1. Raymond C. Rosen et al., "The Multinational Men's Attitudes to Life Events and Sexuality (Males) Study: I. Prevalence of Erectile Dysfunction and Related Health Concerns in the General Population," *Current Medical Research and Opinion* 20, no. 5 (2004): 607–17, https://doi.org/10.1185/030079904125003467.
2. For instance, clinical trials of antidepressant use aimed at improving confidence and self-esteem and lowering anxiety levels also were found to directly improve erectile dysfunction. Stanley E. Althof et al., "Self-Esteem, Confidence, and Relationships in Men Treated with Sildenafil Citrate for Erectile Dysfunction: Results of Two Double-Blind, Placebo-Controlled Trials," *Journal of General Internal Medicine* 21, no. 10, (October 2006): 1069–1074, https://doi.org/10.1111/j.1525-1497.2006.00554.x.
3. Recovery time greatly varies dependent on the frequency of porn use, how long porn had been used, and the age when porn use started. Many anecdotal reports of recovering sexual function and desire proliferate on online forums, most famously by actor Terry

Crews. But clinical reports of the efficacy of quitting porn are also emerging in medical literature, such as this: Brian Y. Park et al., "Is Internet Pornography Causing Sexual Dysfunctions? A Review with Clinical Reports," *Behavioral Sciences* 6, no. 3 (June 2018): 55, https://doi.org/10.3390/bs6030017. In our surveys, we also found that men who had once used porn but now had quit had similar rates of sexual performance and satisfaction than men who had not used porn.

4. For more information, see "What Is Premature Ejaculation?," Urology Care Foundation, July 16, 2020, https://www.urologyhealth.org/urology-a-z/p/premature-ejaculation.

5. "Low Testosterone Reference Summary," The Patient Education Institute, 2009, http://www.nlm.nih.gov/medlineplus/tutorials/lowtestosterone/ur189102.pdf.

6. Robert Rister, "Top Reasons for Low Libido: Sex Drive Killers," *Men's Health*, December 26, 2017, https://www.steadyhealth.com/articles/top-reasons-for-low-libido-sex-drive-killers. Other studies have also found that excess weight leads to lower testosterone, thus affecting libido. Mark Ng Tang Fui, Philippe Dupuis, and Mathis Grossmann, "Lowered Testosterone in Male Obesity: Mechanisms, Morbidity and Management," *Asian Journal of Andrology* 16, no. 2 (2014): 223–31, https://doi.org/10.4103/1008-682X.122365.

7. Rister, "Top Reasons for Low Libido."

8. Andrew J. Bauman, "A Pornographic Style of Relating," AndrewJBauman.com, October 1, 2016. https://andrewjbauman.com/a-pornographic-style-of-relating/.

Chapter 10: The Sex Cycle

1. Ekaterina Mitricheva et al., "Neural Substrates of Sexual Arousal Are Not Sex Dependent," *Proceedings of the National Academy of Sciences* 116, no. 31 (July 2019): 15671–76, https://doi.org/10.1073/pnas.1904975116.

2. Michael Castleman, "Desire in Women: Does It Lead to Sex? Or Result from It?," *Psychology Today*, July 15, 2009, http://www

.psychologytoday.com/blog/all-about-sex/200907/desire-in-women
-does-it-lead-sex-or-result-it.

3. Sheila Wray Gregoire, Joanna Sawatsky, and Rebecca Gregoire
Lindenbach, *The Great Sex Rescue: The Lies You've Been Taught and
How to Recover What God Intended* (Grand Rapids: Baker, 2020), 133.

4. Markham Heid, "Here's How Much Sex You Should Have Every
Week," *Time*, March 7, 2017, https://time.com/4692326/how-much
-sex-is-healthy-in-a-relationship/.

5. For complete results of how feeling obligated to have sex affects
marital and sexual satisfaction, see *The Great Sex Rescue*, pages
174–75.

6. Also, consent is vital in marriage. If he is insisting on sex multiple
times a day and makes you feel inadequate if you don't give in to
his demands, that is a form of coercion. Please talk to a licensed
counselor, or if you're in imminent danger, please call a domestic
violence hotline.

Appendix 1: How to Have an Amazing Honeymoon

1. The book was *The Act of Marriage* by Tim and Beverly LaHaye.

2. C. S. Lewis, *The Four Loves* (Glasgow: William Collins & Sons,
1960), 95.

3. For this statistic, we controlled for prior abuse, so that was not a
confounding factor. We compared women who had had sex for
the first time after the wedding with those who had had sex before
the wedding, but only with the person they were now married to.
Vaginismus rates were lower if sex had occurred before marriage.

4. For instance, women who believe the "obligation sex" message—
that they must have sex whenever their husbands want it—are
39 percent more likely to suffer from vaginismus. When women
feel as if sex is not something they freely choose, our bodies often
rebel, almost in a trauma-like response. If this continues past the
honeymoon, seek out a pelvic floor physiotherapist.

The Good Guy's Guide to Great Sex

Because Good Guys Make the Best Lovers

Sheila Wray Gregoire and Dr. Keith Gregoire

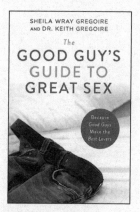

If you ever wonder, "Is this all there is to sex?" or "I wish I knew how to help my wife enjoy this more," you'll appreciate this straightforward, helpful, and faith-based advice on how to have a better sex life.

Based on groundbreaking surveys of more than twenty-five thousand people, this highly practical, research-based book shows guys how to rock their wife's world. The *Good Guy's Guide to Great Sex* from popular marriage blogger and speaker Sheila Wray Gregoire and her husband, Dr. Keith Gregoire, will help you:

- Discover what your wife wants most from you in the bedroom
- Realize what can derail a couple's sex life and how to get it back on track
- Find healing from past trauma, previous relationships, and porn addiction
- Understand your own sex drive and how to keep it revved
- Learn the secrets to giving your wife the most fulfilling sex she's ever had

Available in stores and online!

31 Days to Great Sex

Love. Friendship. Fun.

Sheila Wray Gregoire

This practical book provides 31 days of challenges to help you and your spouse talk, flirt, and explore all three levels of sexual intimacy—physical, emotional, and spiritual—so you both can experience the best sex ever.

Sex is incredibly important in a marriage, yet many things can throw it off course. Whether you are engaged and afraid you won't be able to light the spark, are newlyweds who haven't started off well, or have been married five, ten, twenty-five years, or more and you'd like to recapture the spark you once had, this book is for you!

The challenges aim to spice up the bedroom while guiding you through all three levels of sexual intimacy. As you go through these challenges with lots of laughter and enjoyment, sex will stop being a source of tension and become something fun that brings you together, just the way God intended.

The challenges slowly build on each other to help you:

- Turn sex into something positive
- Understand each other's sexual drives
- Debunk Hollywood myths and expectations about sex
- Hit the reset button on your sex life
- Make little changes that have big rewards
- Try new things and spice things up
- And keep the momentum going!

You're meant to have an abundant marriage—so don't settle for mediocre. Start your 31-day journey today!

Available in stores and online!

ZONDERVAN®
.com